Tactics in Counseling and Psychotherapy

Tactics in Counseling and Psychotherapy

Harold H. Mosak

Adler School of Professional Psychology

Michael P. Maniacci

Adler School of Professional Psychology

F.E. Peacock Publishers, Inc.
Itasca, Illinois

To Birdie...*awlehaw hasholom*
Her door was never closed.
No one ever left her house hungry.

—Harold Mosak

To my first psychotherapy teachers, to whom I owe so much:

Harold H. Mosak
James DelGenio
David Taussig

—Michael Maniacci

Copyright © 1998
F.E. Peacock Publishers, Inc.
All rights reserved
Library of Congress Catalog Card No. 98-65651
ISBN 0-87581-417-4
Printed in the U.S.A.
Printing: 10 9 8 7 6 5 4 3 2 1
Year: 03 02 01 00 99 98

Contents

Preface

Students engaged in the process of learning the practice of counseling and psychotherapy are generally taught a therapeutic philosophy and a strategy for the conduct of psychotherapy. They are taught that they must be warm, accepting, and permissive, and must demonstrate unconditional positive regard. They must manage the transference and work through the client's resistance. Lifestyle must be changed and social interest developed. Action techniques are held to be preferable to verbal interventions—or *vice versa*; and behavioral change must be accompanied by insight, or it can occur in the absence of insight. The message is that we ought to strive to help people change their behaviors or feelings or cognitions or goals or interpersonal behavior or physiological responses and other similar variables.

Each system of therapy offers its "philosophy of salvation" (sometimes even designating those elected for salvation in the form of prognostic indications) and a long-range method, often couched in abstract terms for attaining salvation (Mosak, 1990). Yet repeatedly, students—new and old—ask themselves, their teachers, and their supervisors questions in the form of "What do you do when the patient...?" Their concern lies not with what to do in the long range but what to do at a particular moment in the therapeutic encounter to get past some sticky point.

Thus, what do you do if the patient is reluctant? What do you do if the patient remains silent? Is assaultive? Is constantly tardy?

Is resistive? If the patient has insight, how do you help him or her to change? How do you get what you want across to the patient in a way that it will be accepted? How do you help the depressive to relinquish the depression? In each instance, the inquirer requests an immediate intervention, a tactic that will carry the therapy forward.

The distinction between strategies and tactics first occurred to the senior author (HM) while studying nondirective therapy with Carl Rogers and his group at the University of Chicago immediately after World War II. At that time, the therapist was instructed to establish a warm, permissive, acceptant atmosphere and to reflect the client's feelings. Simultaneously, HM was an intern at a large Veterans Administration hospital, working with many psychotic patients, one of them a mute catatonic schizophrenic. There is a hoary psychological joke that "therapy is an encounter between two people, one called the therapist and one called the patient. The anxious one is the patient." In those days, this ran counter to the author's experience. Since nondirective therapy permitted no use of tactics, HM sat there looking at the client in his warmest, most permissive and acceptant manner, and the client sat silently. The client appeared to be calm; the therapist was the anxious one.

The distinction between strategies and tactics was later revivified when HM served on teams administering specialty board examinations. Since candidates were examined in *their* brand of therapy, we asked them initially about their adherence to some system of psychotherapy. Several candidates replied that they practiced analytically oriented psychotherapy. As the examination progressed, an examiner would often ask, "What was your strategy in the conduct of this psychotherapy?" to which candidates replied, "The management of the transference." Upon receiving such a reply, HM would inquire, "Would you show me how in this interview (or series of interviews) you accomplished that objective?" Apparently those who mentioned transference during the examination used the concept only in nominalistic fashion. On no occasion was a candidate able to demonstrate it. Those who could actually implement the concept in practice rarely mentioned it by name. Those candidates who knew how to manage the transference apparently never mentioned it, and those who didn't tried to mask their ignorance by giving the "right" answer.

As the years progressed and the number of students HM taught and supervised multiplied, he was impressed by the minimal exposure that students have to the study of tactics. Often in academic departments (with their emphasis upon research*), students are better acquainted with the literature than they are with the "What do I do when..." *tactics* available to them when they are engaged in psychotherapy. This is not to minimize the importance of having a strategy in psychotherapy, nor in our opinion does it invalidate the need for the therapist to rely upon some theory or system of psychotherapy. Neither are we ignoring the importance of other factors in psychotherapy such as relationship issues, communication style and problems, and the employment of adjunctive media. This book is an attempt merely to focus upon one often-neglected topic in the study of psychotherapy.

The tactics discussed are not intended to be all-inclusive but to be illustrative of the variety of methods that some creative therapists have utilized in meeting some of the tactical problems encountered in psychotherapy. Many of the tactics emerged as a result of our teaching and our having done multiple psychotherapy with Adlerians and therapists of other orientations. Further, we have not included tactics that we have not found successful in practice. While such a comprehensive treatment might spare therapists some unsuccessful attempts, the corpus of unsuccessful tactics might easily exceed that of effective ones. On the other hand, the reader should not assume that these omissions indicate that everything in our repertoire always works. While some of the tactics are the authors', many are based upon observations of other therapists with whom we have had the good fortune to study and work, most notably Rudolf Dreikurs, Erwin O. Krausz, and Bernard H. Shulman. To them and many others, thanks.

We will be using the words "client" and "patient" interchangeably in this volume. Partly this practice has its origins in HM's internship experience, in which he was a Rogerian student

---

*Certainly we are not minimizing the need for and value of research in psychotherapy. Even psychotherapists who do not engage in research themselves might profit from an acquaintanceship with the research literature.

at the University of Chicago, while practicing Freudian-oriented psychotherapy at his VA internship site. He counseled "clients" at the former and treated "patients" at the latter.

And, finally, the examples used throughout this book are real, but we have disguised the identity of individuals so as to protect confidentiality.

ACKNOWLEDGMENTS

We would like to thank three people for all their help with the preparation of this work. First, Karen Sulikowski and John Czupowski did wonders for us in helping to tame that most important but often unfathomable monster, the COMPUTER. Thank you both for all your patience and help. Second, thank you to Lucia Kelly for her assistance in typing parts of the manuscript.

1

Guidelines for the Use of Tactics

Theodore Reik, in his book on psychotherapy entitled *Listening with the Third Ear* (1948), discusses why he waited until so late in life and so long into his professional career before he wrote his first book on psychotherapy. He replied (to paraphrase) that first, he had not made all the errors he was going to make. Second, he had not yet made them often enough....

Every psychotherapy has some implicit guidelines for its conduct. Tactics do not emerge off the top of the therapist's head, although they often appear to do so. Tactics have their roots in theory, in the therapist's personal style, and in the therapist's personal philosophy. Although most of these guidelines apply to strategies, following are some that may be applied primarily to the use of tactics.

YOU WILL SURVIVE

Many therapists, especially young, inexperienced ones and "true believers," either limit their ability to function therapeutically or create anxiety for themselves by viewing therapy as based upon a system of rules about which the last word has been said. They are often fond of quoting the giants of their schools, and they proceed as they do because "that's the way I was taught" or "that's the way my supervisor did it." Since these therapists often develop the conviction that there is only one right way to conduct therapy or to intervene, if the "one right way" proves ineffective with a particular patient, they do not even look for a backup approach. Their behavior often reflects the notion that "one false step and you're dead." Experiencing these anxieties, they deprive themselves of the opportunity to proceed spontaneously and creatively. When an intervention misses the mark or patients do not respond in expected ways, the therapist may feel lost or experience panic. YOU WILL SURVIVE!

YOUR CLIENT WILL SURVIVE TOO

Many schools of psychotherapy view the client as fragile, someone who is liable to break at any moment. However, psychotherapy is a cumulative process, not a series of one-time incidents. "Cure" or successful treatment is not effected with one or two "magically potent" phrases or interventions. Just as one or two interventions will not take away all the ills of the client, neither will one or two interventions totally "ruin" the client. While therapists must behave responsibly, they need not and will not achieve perfection. You show respect for the client by not treating him or her as fragile, but as one who can take it (Fromm-Reichman, 1950).

At the same time, respect for the client does not give license to the therapist to do anything she or he feels like doing merely because the client will likely survive. One must remember "primum non nocere"—"Above all, do no harm."

ALWAYS STAY IN MOTION

As therapy is often taught, there is only one response, or one best response, in any given situation. In multiple-choice examinations, students educated in this manner are provided with a patient's statement followed by four or five responses or interventions, only one of which is correct. So trained, they adopt this posture in the therapeutic situation and seek the one (or one best) response. Failing to find this "correct" response in a clinical situation, the therapist is "dead." However, possessing the response and discovering that it was ineffective leaves the therapist in a similar position. For example, a psychiatric resident relates how he "blew" an interview. He and his patient were discussing a topic when "out of nowhere" the patient asked, "Say, Doc, how many times a week do *you* screw *your* wife?" The resident continues,

> My first impulse was to tell him, "None of your business." However, since I believe in an egalitarian therapy, my second feeling was that I should tell him. After all, I had asked him how many times a week he screwed *his* wife. My third feeling was the same as the first—"None of your business." By this time the patient was delighted with my discomfort, so I terminated the interview and took him back to the ward.

It never occurred to the resident to simply inquire, "Why would you like to know?" This response and other responses might have been available to the therapist if he had studied with the senior author's (HM) World War II Air Force jiujitsu instructor.

At the first lesson, the teacher offered a preface to breaking holds placed by the opponent. "Before I teach you any specific breaks for holds, I'd like you to know this: If someone gets you in a hold, wiggle, bend, pull, scratch, elbow, bite—*always stay in motion*. If you stop moving, you're dead." It is much the same in psychotherapy. If one tactic, response, or interpretation does not work, the therapist should be searching for another. For the therapist it invites creativeness. For both therapists and clients it also accelerates therapy, because when therapists arrive at this point of discomfort—accompanied by feelings of awkwardness and perhaps even of self-denigration—they are usually paying more attention to themselves than they are to their clients. Becoming aware of this focus, therapists can turn their eyeballs back outward, and while they may not know exactly what to do, they can rest secure in that there is usually something that can be done. As Dreikurs (personal communication) would inform his students who would tell him, "I just had nothing to say at that moment," "There's always something you can say. If nothing else, you can say, 'Gee, I don't know what to say.'" Then, instead of devoting themselves to their own negative feelings, they can place themselves in a position to seek out or create a solution to the problem.

It is also true that prognosis often involves adopting a pessimistic stance. What success might a therapist anticipate if confronted, in a previous era, with a patient who was a "constitutional psychopathic inferior"? And does not prognosis often lead to a self-fulfilling prophecy? When he was an intern, HM had a supervisor who revealed how he kept his hospital caseload within manageable proportions. "One-third are schizophrenic and can't enter a transference relationship; one-third are psychopaths with poor prognosis; the other one-third I treat."

BELIEVING IS SEEING

The self-fulfilling prophecy is very relevant to this guideline: An optimistic stance on the part of the therapist will produce better results than a pessimistic one. As Adler (1932/1964b) pointed out, what you believe will determine what you do. If the therapist believes that there is no way out, then most likely there will be no way out. Therapeutic optimism applies not only to the *client's* chances, but to the *therapist's* skills as well.

CREATIVITY VERSUS GIMMICKRY

The difference between someone who uses "gimmicks" and a creative therapist influences the way in which the choice of tactics is made. A gimmicky therapist uses tactics as ends in themselves, not as a means to an end. The creative therapist knows what tactic to use, why it and not another one should be used at that time, and where it will lead in therapy. To avoid gimmickry, we will supply a rationale for each tactic used.

NEVER PLAY THE PATIENT'S GAME

Adler (1956) and Berne (1964) spoke of the dangers of getting caught up in the client's "game." Many clients, in order to deal with the stresses of life and interpersonal interactions, have developed patterns of behaving and interacting at which they have become "experts." The clients' "style of life" or "game" or "script" has been studied, practiced, and perfected for many years in many different settings with many different types of people, and any therapist who attempts to "beat" a client at his or her own game is asking for trouble. The client knows the rules and maneuvers of the game intimately, and the therapist must be careful not to get "caught up" in such a situation. At the patient's game, the patient is a "pro" and the therapist is an amateur. Under these conditions the likely outcome is predictable.

NO TACTIC IS A PANACEA

Like the futile search in chemistry for the universal solvent, the search for a tactic that is universally effective, "curing" all patients under any and all conditions, brings us similarly to a dead end. Tactics, when they are effective, are effective only in terms of a particular theoretical position, for a particular therapist, a particular client, and a particular stage (or even moment) in therapy. It follows that the therapist cannot apply tactics in mechanical or cookbook fashion. While many tactics are applicable to a broad spectrum of therapeutic conditions, others may be used only once in a therapist's lifetime. Whatever the range of application may be, a specific tactic, like any other therapeutic intervention, may not "work." If it does not, stay in motion.

It should be further understood that a tactic does not exist as a substitute for psychotherapy, or as an equivalent of psychotherapy. Tactics are not the whole of therapy; therapy consists of more than the application of one "gimmick" after another. While the tactic may move the patient/therapy out of a rut, it must usually be accompanied by discussion, clarification, understanding, interpretation, warmth, acceptance of the client, and whatever other procedures the therapist may utilize—in the establishment and maintenance of the relationship and in the creation of a therapeutic atmosphere.

NO TACTIC IS A CURE

A tactic is not a cure, but rather, it is something that moves the therapist and patient past a certain point. Getting a depressed person to smile and laugh will not necessarily "solve" all problems and cure the depression, but it will allow progress to be made toward the alleviation of the depression. Helping someone to resolve a conflict will not alter the issues that led to the conflict initially, but will move the client and therapy along.

KNOW YOUR THEORY

In a paper entitled, "Are Psychological Schools of Thought Outdated?" Dreikurs (1960/1987) formulated the arguments for preserving the tradition of adhering to some psychological theory, some underlying assumptions, some model of human nature, even if these are not stated as formal statements. In the utilization of tactics, knowledge of one's theory becomes essential since this knowledge permits the avoidance of tactics that violate the therapist's philosophy. For example, nondirective therapists will read this book only out of academic interest, since their therapeutic philosophy precludes the use of tactics because, by definition, tactics are directive. Moreover, while eclecticism may be a defensible point of view for some, the indiscriminate use of tactics may reflect the therapist's ignorance rather than flexibility of approach. Some years ago, HM served on a team designated to examine a psychologist in the field of psychotherapy. When asked his orientation, the latter replied, "nondirective therapy and hypnosis." The response was somewhat reminiscent of the apocryphal story about Freud's and Adler's agreement regarding American psychiatrists' thought processes. According to this story, American psychiatrists think that "chocolate is very good to eat. Garlic is also very good. Therefore, the very best food you can eat is chocolate-covered garlic." An unthought-out philosophical position presents similar dangers.

KNOW YOUR PATIENT

There is no substitute for a thorough understanding of your patient. Simply stating that "He is a controller" or that "She has penis envy" is not sufficient. Nomothetic (i.e., general) principles are useful for teaching and communicating to other professionals, but the idiographic, particular aspects of the client's situation need to be thoroughly understood. Many clinicians have had the tedious task of reading through pages of psychological reports or case studies that could have been written about virtually any client at any given time. Tallent (1958) refers to these as "Aunt Fanny reports" because they could describe anyone's "Aunt Fanny." A specific, clear understanding of what makes *this* client "tick" (not just "sick") will greatly enhance the success of any tactic. Unfortunately, many therapists occupy themselves more often with searching for pathology rather than attempting to understand the client.

Knowing your client also implies knowing something about your client's religious, ethnic, and cultural background. In this age of multicultural awareness and sensitivity, clinicians need to be respectful of various dynamics beyond "intrapsychic" forces and processes. Given that caveat, we are not necessarily emphasizing tactics that are based upon multicultural dynamics per se, as much as we are discussing tactics that are situation specific. We will not emphasize assorted cultural issues as much as the situation in which clients and therapists find themselves, and what can be done at a particular time in a particular context. When certain religious, or cultural, dynamics are of particular importance, of course those factors should be considered.

UNDERSTANDING TIMING

A tearful, depressed client relating a sensitive, personal issue will not be receptive to a forceful, confrontational tactic. Moreover, anxiety-producing tactics are probably not appropriate for the very first minutes of an initial interview. What tactic to use with what client is important; when to use it is equally important (Mosak & Shulman, 1974, 1977). It has been said often that the essence of good comedy is timing—knowing *when* to use the right word/phrase/gesture in the right way in order to elicit the desired response, laughter. Much the same can be said about counseling and psychotherapy. Many a novice therapist has wasted breath and energy by presenting interpretations that, though accurate, were given too soon, before the client was "ready" to hear them. HM refers to this readiness as "ripeness." Being attuned to the timing of interventions will greatly improve their effectiveness and assure that the therapist and client are aligned in their transactions.

BE COMFORTABLE WITH WHAT YOU DO

If you are not comfortable with what you do, do not do it. Tactics are most effective when you believe in them and in your ability to use them. Clients will sense the therapist's discomfort and react accordingly. After practice and a few attempts, if you are still not comfortable with a tactic, forget it. As Freud (1958) wrote, "No psychoanalyst goes further than his own complexes and internal resistances permit" (p. 145). Everyone is limited to some extent and will not feel comfortable with everything.

DEVELOP YOUR OWN STYLE—DON'T MIMIC

Believe in yourself. Confidence in a tactic is important, but self-confidence is crucial. How someone else uses a tactic is useful for instructional purposes, but you must apply it in your own unique way. Belief in self is independent of evidence. If you believe in yourself, then you will find the "facts" to support that belief. Fitting a tactic into your particular style will improve its effectiveness, but what works with one therapeutic style may not work with another.

IGNORE ALL THE PREVIOUS "GUIDELINES"

As Adler (1956) repeatedly emphasized, do not follow anyone blindly, not even him. Guidelines are just that—"guidelines." They do not replace clinical judgment, experience, or common sense. If, as Adler said, "Everything can be different" (p. 364), then strict adherence to rules or regulations such as those outlined above *cannot and should not be expected to apply in every situation.* Like it or not, psychotherapists must "think on their feet." As Harris (1977) has so succinctly put it, "You have not even begun to master an activity—whether it be playing bridge or statesmanship—until you know when and why a rule not only should be, but must be, broken." In this manner, both therapy and practice evolve.

TACTICS AND THE ISSUE OF MANIPULATING CLIENTS

Before describing the tactics themselves, one brief discussion is in order—about the issue of tactics and manipulation. As Dreikurs (1960/1987) maintained, all psychotherapy involves manipulation; it is just that some schools of thought acknowledge it more openly than others. To assume that the psychotherapist or counselor is not directing or influencing the patient or the process is ludicrous; it is like saying that two people who, sitting in the same room, are not communicating something to one another even if they are not conversing or that one person can communicate to someone without the other person's communicating back [see Haley (1963) for a more detailed discussion of the directive nature of all psychotherapy, even psychoanalysis]. Research has also established the reinforcing qualities of such old "nondirective" comments as "um hum" (Greenspoon, 1955).

Manipulation, explicit and subtle, occurs in psychotherapy. It is a fact. With that accepted as a given, the issue then is threefold: What is the goal the client is being manipulated toward? Is it for the patient's benefit or to merely gratify the therapist's need? Second, the goal of every psychotherapy is to move or help move the patient from here to there; however, "here" and "there" are defined by any system, be it intrapsychic harmony, elimination of games, self-actualization, or changing basic mistakes and encouraging social interest. This is an issue of strategy and philosophy. Third, how does the psychotherapist achieve those goals? That is an issue of *tactics*—the question that this book addresses.

The issue of "manipulation of clients" raises several other dynamics that need to be addressed. How is this book to be used? Is it a "cookbook"?

HOW TO USE THIS BOOK

Every counseling or psychotherapy session is a fluid process that has three parts: the patient, the therapist, and the situation. Let us elaborate. A patient comes into the session at a particular time, with a particular issue, and meets a therapist who also is coming from a particular time and with certain issues. Ideally, the client's issue is something he or she wants changed, and the therapist can assist. This book is about such situations. It is not about clients nor is it about therapists; it is about the *interface* between the therapists and clients, that is, the situations they find themselves in. A glance at the table of contents reveals that we are addressing situations. Except for linguistic purposes, rarely do we write about patients who "have" certain problems. Therapists and patients find themselves in certain situations that need "management," "repair" or whatever term happens to be in vogue at the time. Situations do occur; how we manage them becomes the focus of this book.

As has been mentioned, this is not a theoretical text. There are plenty of other books available that discuss and explore the theory of counseling and psychotherapy. This is intended as a supplement, to help therapists get "past" certain situations.

"Postmodernism" is finding its way into psychotherapy and counseling. While far from a unified system, it has a general orientation that can be summarized (admittedly in broad terms): Clients have life stories that counselors and therapists listen to. The clinicians' task is not to impose order or an outside structure to the clients' story as much as it is to help clients better articulate and decide for themselves if their story is what they want. Given such a perspective, a book of tactics becomes rather unnecessary, for it implies that the clinicians are setting themselves up as "experts" upon clients and their lives. Well, there is some validity to such a point, and we never want to be in that kind of control of anybody's life. Yet, it is not so simple a matter. Let us elaborate.

Throughout our experience, we have found that there are few if any universals in life. As noted previously, when we said, "know when to disregard the rules," flexibility is required, not just in life, but in counseling and therapy as well. The postmodern emphasis upon "mutual exploration" is certainly valid and worthwhile, some of the time; but not all clients and not all situations can be approached from such a perspective. Some clients, in some situations, require a more active, directive stance on the part of the clinician. Not to consider such a stance, even occasionally, is to put theoretical premises above clinical utility. We too, as counselors and therapists, need flexibility. One way of managing such a stance, as we advocate in this book, is to approach clients with the following declaration:

> I am an expert in psychology. You are an expert in you. I can only "put us in the ballpark," so to speak, but you must "take us home." Feel free to elaborate, change, or correct anything I say at any time. I will make assumptions—as any person does—but in here, I will often share my assumptions about you and our situation with you, so I can get your feedback. Feel free to work with me. We both will find it more satisfying and a lot more productive if you do.

We do strongly believe that while therapists and counselors should not control patients (again, there are some admittedly rare but important exceptions to such a stance), therapists and counselors should always be in charge of the *process* of counseling and psychotherapy. We advocate professionally trained and clinically competent counselors and psychotherapists. To receive such training and supervision and then act as if such training was not needed is to subscribe to the assumption that no training is needed. There may be times the clinician may want to act "as if" this was the case, but, as we will discuss, that is a role the therapist uses, not a stance he or she consistently maintains. Professionally trained counselors and therapists are just those—professionals, and they should not be afraid of having more training and expertise in some areas than their clients do. We can control the process without controlling the person. In our opinion, that is what all the training and supervision is about.

Once again, this book is not designed to replace experience, training, supervision, or a solid grounding in theory. It is to supplement such backgrounds that we write. There are probably more instances when we do not use the tactics discussed than there are when we do, but it is nice to know there are tactics that can be used in such situations at such times. One may never have to use a jack to change a tire, but we would not recommend driving without knowing how to use one or where to find one, should the situation arise. It can even be argued that the postmodern approach is advocating one type of tactic, albeit a common-sense one—that of listening and being supportive. We advocate the use of such a tactic too (see Chapter 9, "Encouragement Tactics"), simply not all the time in every situation.

2

Differential Diagnostic Techniques

Not every psychotherapist is medically trained. In increasing numbers, psychologists, clinical social workers, and counselors are becoming involved in the art and science of psychotherapy. Even those therapists who possess a medical background do not always have at their disposal the required tests and procedures/ facilities* in order to engage in a full-scale medical evaluation. As is becoming increasingly true with the ever-growing trend toward medical specialization, not every psychiatrist is comfortable with doing such required examinations after spending a few years in the practice of psychotherapy.

A helpful distinction is called for before proceeding any further. Any major complaint that has a physical component to it should be seriously evaluated. Although referral to a physician may not be always indicated, some experts recommend a regular checkup by a physician every year regardless of the individual's health status. If it has been more than a year since the last physical examination, it may be wise to request one of clients at the beginning of therapy. Even if no physical complaint is present, it communicates a helpful message. Clients, as people, are being

---

*Consider Berne's (1964) game of "Bulgarian peasant."

dealt with, and not just their symptoms, complexes, or psycho-dynamics. They are cared for as more than "patients"; they are treated as individuals. A message about the level of competency of the therapist is being communicated as well. Psychotherapists are not magicians and are neither omnipotent nor omniscient. They should not try to be. The tactics presented here should be read with these *caveats* in mind—and one other as well. These tactics are used to identify potential problems, not diagnose them. Therapists should be able to identify potential problems, even if diagnosis is not practical.

THE QUESTION

Psychotherapists are often faced with two decisions with respect to differential diagnosis. The first involves distinguishing between so-called somatogenic and psychogenic conditions. The second involves distinguishing between psychological conditions and medical conditions whose symptoms mimic those of psychopathological conditions. Under the medical model, the major approach to differential diagnosis is to refer the client for a medical examination, a procedure that often falls short of detecting existing medical conditions. It involves diagnosis through exclusion. If one scrutinizes medical charts, one often sees a statement such as "R/O cardiovascular disease." Using this approach, the physician rules out—many times through tests—certain conditions that may have a symptom that the patient describes. When the physician rules out the physical conditions, he or she may inform the patient that "It's all in your mind," or "You've got a case of nerves," and perhaps prescribe some sedative or tranquilizer. However, excluding these ruled-out conditions does not guarantee that a physical condition does not exist; it merely indicates that one has not been found. Consequently, it is possible for the person to have an undiscovered or undiagnosed physical condition. Under these circumstances, if clients are treated through psychotherapy, there will be little or no improvement. They may be treated for a condition they do not have, while the condition they do have remains undiagnosed and untreated.

For those therapists who do not subscribe to the medical model of psychotherapy, Adler (1956) has made available another approach—diagnosis on the basis of purpose. Simply stated, Adler held that all behavior had a purpose. Symptoms, being behavior, therefore have purposes (Shulman & Mosak, 1967). He further suggested that somatogenic symptoms have a physical purpose and that psychogenic symptoms have a psychological or social purpose. To illustrate, a fever may have the purpose of mobilizing the body's defenses, and it may also signal that some disease is present. Witness the mother's method of "diagnosing" her child by placing her hand on the child's forehead. If it is warm to the touch, the child stays home from school; if it is not, then the child may be sent to school. Taking advantage of these hypotheses, Adler (1929/1964a) and Dreikurs (1958, 1962) introduced "The Question." We ask, "If I were to give you a magic pill (or wave a magic wand) and remove all your symptoms immediately and forever, what would be different in your life?"* If the client responds with a statement such as "I just wouldn't be in pain all the time," the symptom is *most likely* somatogenic. On the other hand, if the client answers with a statement such as "I'd write that book I've always been meaning to write" or "I'd be able to get married," then we assume the symptom to be psychogenic.

As with other diagnostic techniques, medical and psychological, "The Question" is not foolproof. There are people who give *both* types of response. When this occurs, both somatic *and* psychologic components are present. For example, there are people who have psychological conditions with somatic overlays (e.g., the catatonic who stands endlessly on a line on the floor and develops an edema in his ankles) and there are physical conditions with psychological overlays (e.g., the person who, in his anxiety after a myocardial infarction, walks around with his ear glued to his heartbeat). Nevertheless, with these exceptions and cautions kept in mind, the tactic is highly effective (Mosak, 1977, 1995). Brown (1995) was able to predict correctly the somatic versus the psychologic in more than 90 percent of his cases.

---

*Adler's wording was "What would be different in your life if you didn't have this problem?"

A woman came to see HM. A brief interview made it clear she was obviously schizophrenic. While some time was spent reviewing her symptoms, previous treatments, and history, she (almost off-handedly) mentioned that she had a long history of headaches. When asked "The Question," she replied that "My head wouldn't hurt." This was significant: Her headaches were probably somatic. She was referred to a physician who sent her back, saying she was clearly schizophrenic. Once again, she was returned to her physician, who assured her that she needed to "speak to her therapist," and not to worry about her headaches. This transaction went on several times, with more than one physician. Finally she was brought to a colleague, a dentist, who specialized in headaches. The senior author met her at the office of the dentist, who had her stand up against a wall, and asked HM to look at her. She was clearly "out of balance"; that is, her right shoulder was several inches higher than her left. The dentist felt her headaches were a result of her posture, and told her that she needed heel pads. "Oh, heel pads, I've got one of those!" she excitedly declared. When asked to see it, she took it out of her right shoe. She had been diagnosed correctly years earlier, but had used the pad on the wrong heel.

SERIAL SEVENS SUBTRACTION TEST

There are many ways of distinguishing between neurological and psychological symptoms. The neurological examination may be one. In the recent past, neuropsychologists have developed batteries of tests for neurological deficits. Many psychologists use the "tried and true" instruments they were taught in their training like the Bender-Gestalt, the Halstead-Reitan, and the Luria-Nebraska. Many psychotherapists, however, may not wish to expose all their patients to such testing, given the costs, time, and inconvenience of the process. A rapid screening device was needed, which Hayman (1942) developed. The Serial Sevens Subtraction Test was a product of the period before psychologists had at their disposal sophisticated psychological tests. The client is asked to start with the number 100, then instructed to subtract 7, and then 7 again from the new difference, and then 7 again "all the way down."* If you give the patient three runs of the test, the entire procedure may take a total of five minutes. Although potentially influenced by attentional deficits and level of education (Strub & Black, 1993), this is still an effective screening device.

There are three types of errors. Type I, the ordinary subtraction errors, such as 100, 93, 85…, are found in people who might ordinarily do the same in balancing their checkbooks; sometimes among those who like many, many psychology students taking a statistics course (sometimes proudly) announce, "I was never good in math"; and in people who are situationally or chronically anxious. The Type II error consists of substituting another number for 7, such as the number 6, or 10, thus altering the instructions, and then perseverating. A typical run might be 100, 93, 85, 76, 66, 56.… Type II errors are often made by schizophrenics, in addition to those with organic pathology. Clinicians will hardly need to rely upon Type II errors to diagnose schizophrenic conditions. Type III errors involve a failure to "lock in," which can be illustrated using the calculator analogy. If we wish to subtract 2 from 5, we will place a 5 in the calculator, follow it by a minus sign, insert a 2 in the calculator, then either pull a crank or press the "equals" button. Then the calculator should display the correct answer—3. However, suppose we have a defective calculator and, at the moment we insert the equals sign in the calculator, the 5 is "lost" or "pops out." In that event, we are subtracting 2 from an unknown number. Consequently, we do not know what answer the defective calculator might display. In the Type IIIA error, we can still deduce what number may have "popped out," for example, 100, 93, 86, 89, 82.… In the Type IIIB error, the process is unfathomable, as in 100, 93, 78, 49, 22, 0. Type III is the error to be considered in making the decision whether to pursue neurological or neuropsychological investigation, especially if such errors appear in all three runs. If the pattern is consistent in all three runs, neurological investigation is in order. We give three runs to determine whether the patient's performance remains constant, improves, or deteriorates.

---

*A caution for those psychologists who proclaim, "I never was good in math": Do not instruct the patient "all the way down to zero." If you give this instruction erroneously, you may confuse your patient and will misinterpret the results.

A ten-year-old boy was brought in for counseling after having become a "behavior problem" at school. He had attacked, and attempted to strangle, a girl on the playground. Arithmetic was his best subject. When given the Serial Sevens Subtraction Test, he failed it miserably, producing many Type III errors. He was referred for neurological examination, and temporal lobe pathology was found—for which medication was immediately prescribed. His behavior improved dramatically. Counseling continued, however, to help him with how to change his reputation as a "bad boy" at school and with peers and teachers.

3

Conflict Resolution Tactics

According to Adlerian theory, the individual is an indivisible whole (Adler, 1956; Dreikurs, 1953, 1967a). Adler gave his theory the name Individual Psychology to emphasize this holistic perspective, with the term *Individual* deriving from the Latin *individuum*, meaning "indivisible." Classical psychoanalytic doctrine views conflict as intrapsychic, between a person's id and ego or id and superego. This notion of intrapsychic conflict is not consonant with Adlerian theory (Mosak & LeFevre, 1976). It is reductionistic rather than holistic. An example of the purposeful nature of conflict will clarify the Adlerian perspective.

A client comes in and says, "I'm in conflict. I have a wife and a girlfriend." He proceeds to add that he "loves them both equally."

The therapist remarks, "Well, if you love them both equally, and you say that you must decide because you hurt so much from this conflict, let's see what we can do to resolve it." If the therapist does not understand the purpose of the conflict, he or she will probably start playing the pro and con game. The client lists the pros and cons of each. His wife is loyal but his girlfriend is beautiful. His wife is good but his girlfriend is great in bed. He loves his family and his leaving would hurt his children, but if he gives up his girlfriend, she'll kill herself. After a while, the true nature of the pro and con game becomes clear. The client is a "pro" at "conning" the therapist (and himself). At the end of every session no decision has been made, and the client, by not making a decision, manages to keep both wife and mistress. Not only does he manage to keep both, he looks "noble" in doing so because of how much he appears to suffer through such a painful process. His conflict is the price he nonconsciously chooses to pay for the privilege of having both women.

Mosak and Shulman (1974) have defined insight as "a meaningful experience leading to perceptual change and leading to a change in the line of movement" (p. 42). In other words, the client who gains insight not only perceives things differently, but acts (moves through life) differently. In a holistic psychology, any distinctions between intellectual and emotional insight become superfluous. When a patient makes this distinction—"My head tells me one thing but my heart tells me another" or "I feel it up here but I don't feel it in my gut"—from a holistic viewpoint he or she is indicating the intention not to move. Such patients want to stay "dead center." As Adler (1956) said, one should trust only movement (p. 330). If one does not move, it makes little difference what one knows. The patient will still remain "dead center." This is illustrated in the old story of the boy and his father who were walking down the street and encountered a growling dog. The father said, "Don't worry, son, the dog won't bite. Everyone knows that barking dogs don't bite," to which the son replied as he withdrew anxiously behind the father, "I know that and you know that, but does the dog know that?" Some might say that the boy had experienced a conflict between his emotional insight and his intellectual insight—he knew in his "head" one thing but in his "gut" felt another. The Adlerian would say, "Trust his behavior." He moved behind his father. The boy talked a good game (as many patients do in therapy) in order to please his father, but nonetheless acted according to his real intentions.

Staying "dead center" has certain benefits or payoffs in transactional terminology (Berne, 1964). Let us review some.

1. If a client wants to be right, staying "dead center" is a way of assuring never being wrong. Suffering is the price paid for such security, however. A conflict involves a sense of subjective distress/pain; a decision doesn't. People have to make difficult decisions all the time; that does not imply conflict.

2. Other people are often forced to make the decisions then and potentially even assume the responsibilities.
3. Clients can maintain movement in accordance with their lifestyles, particularly if they are victims or martyrs (Mosak, 1971).
4. Some create conflict to avoid risks. "Better safe than sorry" or "nothing ventured, nothing lost" are their mottos.
5. Clients create conflict at times because it gives them everything they want, such as the aforementioned example of a wife and a girlfriend. In these instances, the conflict isn't *between* "a" and "b," but is a device for having *both* "a" and "b."

If the person is the creator of the conflict because of certain goals, how can she or he be moved from "dead center"? Several ways follow.

THE GAME OF PROBABILITIES

This game is predicated upon the notion that people move in the direction of making their anticipations come true or what Merton (1948) called the "self-fulfilling prophecy." The client is instructed to predict the odds that a particular decision will be reached by some date in the future. The instructions are given this way: "If I were to meet you on the street, say one year from today, on the basis of 100—what are the odds that you would be back with your wife and not seeing the other woman?"* A note of importance: Be sure to use the phrase "on the street" so as to communicate to the client your expectation of improvement. Saying "a year from now in my office" may subtly and iatrogenically imply that you expect the client to be in therapy that length of time. The client's response will reveal in what direction he intends to move. If the client responds that in a year the odds are 75–25 that he'll be back with his wife, then the therapist knows the intentions of the client at a probabilistic level.

The process may then become one of discovering how long the client will wait before making a decision, and altering the time

---

*The time is variable and relative to the situation.

frame may do this. "O.K., what are the odds six months from now?" to which the client responds, "Oh, 60–40." "What are the odds of your going back to your wife three months from today?" the therapist asks, to which the client responds, "50-50"—"dead center" again. In this case the therapist can respond, "Why bug yourself then? You have no intention of going back to your wife for at least three months. Why not enjoy yourself, and after three months, if you retain your current stance, you can start the process of returning to your wife." Frequently, the client, understanding the meaning of the odds, may immediately either change the odds or change the decision, for example, "If that's the case, I might as well return to my wife right now!"

In such a way the therapist has let the client know what his intentions are, and therapeutic efforts can be directed elsewhere, away from the client's "conflict." We can discuss how the decision can be implemented, or the client's fears, or perhaps the lifestyle movement of always creating obstacles or conflicts.

If the client responds that the odds are 50–50, that may deceive some who have studied statistics and assume that 50–50 means equal probabilities. It does in statistics but not in clinical practice. In therapy, 50–50 actually means, "I'm not going to tell you the odds because then I'll know my real intentions and I'm not ready for that yet." The therapist's response to "50–50" can be "I don't know anything, outside of a vacuum balance in a physics laboratory, that is exactly 50–50. It has to be something like 51–49 or 49–51." Pressed this way, the client often replies with a 70–30 or similar answer, revealing that at some level he knows his real intentions but either doesn't want to know them or act upon them. Even a 51–49 answer indicates which way the patient is leaning. Mosak and Maniacci (1995) provide a clinical case example of the use of this tactic with a client.

THE EMPTY CHAIR TECHNIQUE

While it is often considered to be a Gestalt technique (Greenberg, 1979), Shoobs (1946), an Adlerian, is credited with the first reference to this technique in the literature. The tactic is deceptively simple and effective. Two empty chairs are presented to the client, with the instruction to alternately sit in each chair and discuss the pros and cons of each potential decision, with one chair representing the pros and the other the cons. The client is also asked to discuss the feelings associated with the arguments in each chair. In this manner the client arrives at a decision as she or he listens to the arguments and the feelings being tendered. The chair in which the patient is sitting when he or she completes the discussion reflects it. Sometimes, immediately after receiving the instructions, the client declines to proceed and says, "Oh heck, I know what I'm going to do," again revealing his or her knowledge of how the conflict is to be resolved. In other instances the client arrives at a decision but, not infrequently, is sitting in the "wrong" chair for that decision. Again, heeding Adler's words about movement, the therapist should trust the client's nonverbal behavior—that is, the client's line of movement. The chair he or she finally sits in reflects the direction in which the patient is currently planning to move. A schizophrenic patient explained it thus: "As Adler said when constipated, 'Trust only movement.'"

A client at a treatment center approached her therapist with a "conflict." She couldn't decide between studying the piano with a professional tutor (as her mother requested) or continuing to practice on her own, and though she would be quite good, she would never be "polished," especially by her mother's standards. This was typical of the client's lifestyle, constantly "torn" between doing things in her own nonconformist ways and being "submissive," to both her mother specifically and "society" in general. She was given two chairs and the instructions to have one represent taking the lessons (i.e., conforming) and the other, practicing on her own (i.e., rebelling). The client was an intellectualizer, always seeing three sides to every question and four options to each (Mosak & Shulman, 1966), *but rarely moving.* She talked a good game. For almost ten minutes she went off on wonderfully oblique philosophical tangents, all the time moving, albeit reluctantly, between the two chairs, until she finally ended in confusion, successfully managing to cloud the issue and forestall any decision—or so she thought. She ended up in the "no lessons" chair. True to form, that is what she eventually did. Work with this client centered on her ability to complicate and use intellectualization as a safeguarding device (Adler, 1956; Credner, 1936;

Mosak, 1995). The empty chair dramatically pointed out the client's tendency to complicate and obfuscate issues.

This tactic can also be used for exploring "unfinished business" with individuals who are not present or even dead, or the therapist can move into one of the two chairs and initiate more traditional role-playing techniques (Corsini, 1966; Starr, 1977). In either case the empty chair technique can be a useful starting point for either of these other options. If used as in the example provided, it can dramatically demonstrate the old adage that "you can't sit on two chairs with one ass." It reminds psychotherapists that it is not theory, but the act that counts (Hertz, 1958, 1:17). Or, as the apostle James (1:22) stated, "But be ye doers of the Word, and not hearers only."

THE DOUBLE UNBIND

Bateson, Jackson, Haley, and Weakland (1956) described the *double bind* as a situation in which an individual received a communication that expresses two conflicting messages, with one denying the other, leading to disorientation, confusion, and disturbance. Other therapists see this as the lesser of two evils problem, where either choice is difficult or unpleasant. Beecher and Beecher (1966/1971), in discussing Adler's formulation of the concept, describe the double bind as an individual's attempt to "chase two rabbits at once and catching neither" (p. 73). They characterize the conflict of the person experiencing the double bind as rooted in the person's endeavor to please "two masters" (p. 73). Such a stance toward others implies a sense of inferiority and focus upon oneself rather than upon the task at hand. The individual can escape the double bind by focusing attention upon what has to be done, not how he or she is doing in efforts to follow authority. It is task-orientation rather than ego-orientation that should prevail.

A fable tells of the insect that, encountering a centipede, complimented the latter on his coordination and the wonderful way in which his 100 legs moved. He then asked, "Tell me, Mr. Centipede, does the 57th leg move before or after the 32nd?" The poor centipede was stopped dead in his tracks. The moral of the story is "he who watches how he's doing interferes with what he's doing." The moral is highly evident when one is learning to type, play the piano, or drive.

The therapeutic double unbind operates on much the same principles. The patient comes to the therapist and says, "I can't extricate myself from this because I don't like either way it might turn out." It is presented as "Damned if I don't; damned if I do," "between a rock and a hard place," and "between the Devil and the deep blue sea." Again, a lack of movement is attained, which can provide a number of personal benefits. An illustration will demonstrate:

A mother tells the therapist that her daughter's teacher reports that her daughter needs some remedial work and ought to attend summer school. The mother says, "Well, you know she goes to school all year, and I find it difficult to send her to summer school when all the other kids are going to camp. If I send her to school, I will feel guilty taking her recreational time away from her. On the other hand, if I send her to camp with her friends, she won't get the remedial work. She'll go back to school and fall behind and fail. She'll be kept back, missing being with her friends, and I'll feel guilty." She says that she will feel guilty either way. One could play the pro and con game with her but she could marshal arguments that would weight both sides equally. She would remain dead center if that were where she nonconsciously wants to be.

The therapist can place the mother in a double unbind. "You say that in either case you will feel guilty. So the question is not whether your daughter should go to camp; it is which way you prefer to feel guilty." Rather than focusing at this point upon the alleviation of guilt or making the decision for the client, the therapist reframes the situation as one that can be solved if, in this case, accepting the guilt is taken as a given. Allowing that both options are unpleasant, which would the client prefer?

A young schizophrenic client with a similar problem approached a therapist. Thanksgiving Day was upcoming, and he had two choices, neither of which he liked. One was to go with his mother and stepfather to visit family and subsequently experience considerable stress from the situation and probably have hallucinations. The other involved staying at home alone on the holiday, thus avoiding the stressful interactions, but feeling isolated, abandoned, and depressed. This lack of stimulation would probably start him hallucinating, the therapist predicted. The double unbind was presented to him. Where would he prefer hallucinating, at home alone or visiting with his family? He chose to go, and then strategies were planned to cope with the symptoms in as unobtrusive a way as possible.

The double unbind, like the other conflict-reducing tactics, saves considerable time and effort on the part of the therapist as well as reducing the discomfort for the patient. The time and energy saved can be more productively spent on other issues.

COIN FLIPPING

This seems so obvious that it is almost superfluous to include it here, but how it is used is not as obvious as typically thought. If people are in conflict, they are hesitating to move or at least for the time being to make their decision "public," even to the point of not fully or clearly admitting it to themselves. A good test for determining intentions and clarifying movement is to flip a coin. Here is how it works: A woman is undecided and in conflict about whether to accept a new job offer. She is content with her present job but would like to move on to something more challenging. The new job would provide that, which is part of the problem. She is not convinced that she is up to the challenge. While she remains in a state of flux, she manages to have both—the safety of her current job, with its paycheck and known responsibilities, and the excitement of knowing that someone else wants her and considers her capable. She places herself in the position of Hamlet—who wondered whether it is better to "bear those ills we have/Than fly to others that we know not of?"

By flipping the coin, the decision can be made clearer cut. The veil can be lifted from the woman's intentions. The sides of the coin are arbitrarily assigned the two sides of the issue: Heads is for keeping the present job; tails is for taking the new job. The coin is flipped. Two responses are elicited from her. Before she sees which way the coin fell, she is asked what side she thinks it landed on. After she sees how the coin fell, what is her immediate reaction?

The reply to the first question (On which side do you think it landed?) may reveal her intentions. "Tails—I bet it landed on tails and I have to take the new job," she says. She is leaning toward taking the job. By observing her reaction closely and eliciting her immediate reaction upon seeing which side of the coin came up, one can receive further confirmation. "You're right—tails." She looks relieved. "Tell me, what is your first reaction when you say it?" Typically it will be something like relief. If she did not want to see that particular side of the coin, she might say something like, "Oh, no!"

If both sides of the problem were weighted exactly equally, then there would be no problem with accepting the results of the coin toss. The problem would be solved. But if the woman's intentions are leaning toward one or the other solution, it will be revealed by her immediate response to the toss, either through a sense of relief that her "hidden intentions" were confirmed or through some form of displeasure because she did not get the answer that she was seeking.

4

Assuming Another's Perspective

Adler (1956) characterized empathy as the ability to "see with the eyes of another, hear with the ears of another, and feel with the heart of another" (p. 135). The ability to assume such a perspective meant that the individual was able to make use of common sense, that is, to escape the *private logic* she or he developed about self, others, and the world, and instead assume a stance that shared a sense of community (*Gemeinschaftsgefühl*), of interdependence and cooperation with others (Ansbacher, 1965; Mosak, 1991).

The ability to take another's perspective is central. Therapy has been characterized as the client assuming (gradually) the therapist's less rigid and more flexible stance toward life (Mahoney, 1980). Mosak (1950) writes, "Half facetiously this writer once differentiated between nondirective and directive therapies in the following manner. The goal of the former is to get the client to accept his own rationalizations; in the latter he is expected to accept the therapist's rationalizations" (p. 18). Getting the client to take some other person's perspective, be it through role-playing (Corsini, 1966; Starr, 1977) or some other technique, can be very beneficial. An example of this would be the patient who began to have a fear of death at age 36. His litany of complaints all reduced to a "poor me" stance. "I had no father—he died at 36. I grew up without one, and all the kids had fathers to do things with and I had none. They did father and son things." He asked for sympathy, to which the therapist replied, "I don't feel 'poor you' at all. I feel 'poor father'—he only lived until age 36 and never got to see his kids grow up. You'll see your kids grow up, and that's something your father never experienced. So if I'm going to feel sorry for anyone, it's for him, not you." The client burst out crying and said, "I never thought of it like that. I guess I'm pretty lucky." Subsequently, he felt more sorry for his father and less for himself. He no longer played the role of "poor me."

THE HIGHER-STANDARDS-THAN-GOD TACTIC

The arrogance of some clients can reach high proportions. Adler often mentioned that inferiority and superiority were two sides of the same coin, the latter often compensating for the former. A clergyman related to his therapist that he had committed a sin that made him, in his opinion, unfit to continue to function in that role. The therapist inquired whether salvation for sinners existed in his theology. "Of course," he replied. "That would suggest that God could forgive you." "Yes, but *I* can't forgive myself." "Isn't it sad that God has such low standards? He'll forgive anyone, but your standards are much higher."

Another clergyman, one day, used the therapist as a confessor. Behaviorally the man was a saint; yet he complained of urges, inclinations, and temptations he had, although he had never acted upon them. Finally, when he finished, he summarized, "Let's face it; my whole life has consisted of wrestling with the Devil." He sat awaiting a negative verdict from the therapist, who merely said, "If it was good enough for Jesus, I suspect it ought to be good enough for you." The clergyman practically fell out of his chair laughing (Mosak, 1987b).

In a similar variation of this tactic, Mosak and Maniacci (1995) present a case in which the client felt that everybody had to like him; if anyone rejected him, it was devastating. Since this client was also religious, his standards were placed in perspective. Not everyone loves God all the time. If God could be rejected now and then, could the client perhaps also? He, too, found himself laughing at the absurdity of his expectations. This tactic is especially useful with pleasers (Hart, 1977; Mosak, 1971).

Such a tactic places into perspective the client's often unrealistic, and consequently unattainable, goals. To admit such a goal and still adhere to it is something most clients will not do.

LEAVING SOMETHING UNDONE

This technique, while applicable to a variety of clients in a number of different situations, is especially so with persons with obsessive-compulsive personality structures. The compulsive housewife who is up cleaning the ceiling at 2:00 in the morning wants her therapist to agree with her on how important cleanliness is. The therapist may respond by informing her that her goal is futile. "No matter how much time you spend at it and how hard you work at it, the day you die there's going to be some left over. Since that is the case, why not decide what you're going to leave over if you were to die tomorrow? Then handle all the rest." The client in this way is encouraged to lighten up on herself and her workload.

In a similar situation, a therapist employed this tactic with a pleaser. The young man was fearful of displeasing anyone he viewed as an authority figure. Again, he was asked whom, at his death, would he still not be able to please? He responded with a laugh and named his father, to which the therapist replied, "So why not start right now? Since you're never going to please him, why not quit trying today?" That was a turning point in his therapy and in his relationship with his father.

HIERARCHY OF VALUES

A simple way of placing things in perspective is to have clients make lists in descending order of things they value. Those items listed at the top have the highest priority; those listed on the bottom, the lowest. An example of such a list might appear like this:

Values List for John D

1. Health
2. Family (wife and children)
3. Career
4. Money
5. Friends
6. Home

7. Sex
8. Education
9. Politics
10. Appearance
11. Community
12. Religion

A quick glance at this list reveals upon what John consciously places emphasis. He values his health and family first, but career and money are also very high—third and fourth on his list. Issues that are most distressing to him would probably revolve around that top four or five. Sex, education, and religion are low priorities. Obviously, those areas, while still somewhat important (they did make the list), are not really worth investing much of his time. He will be unwilling to fight very hard over such issues or to be more than minimally concerned with them. Therapeutic time, especially if one is conducting brief psychotherapy, might more profitably be spent focusing upon issues that have the most relevance and meaning for the client. Not only does the therapist gain a good understanding of the values, but also the clients are provided with the opportunity to examine and question themselves about these issues.

Sherman and Fredman (1986) describe a useful adjunct of this tactic in couples and family therapy. Each member is requested to create a list, and the lists are compared. If father places an item on his list, such as Career near the top and mother (or anyone else in the family) does not place Career anywhere near the top, then the potential for conflict emerges. He will be investing considerable time and energy into something others in his family do not value as much. If a husband's and wife's lists are very much discrepant, again the potential for conflict is high. If she values Family first and Sex eighth, and he values Sex second and Family sixth, some of the complaints that could be expected from each can be predicted. Therapeutic work can be directed to reaching compromise, establishing contracts, conducting negotiations, and arriving at resolutions for the discrepancies—if the awareness alone is insufficient to reduce tensions.

Sherman and Fredman (1986) also add that asking couples to make a list of their spouse's values can be illuminating as well. In that way, not only are individual values assessed, but also couples are provided the opportunity to test their perceptions of each other's priorities. For example:

Couple A

My Values	My Wife's	My Values	My Husband's
Family	Family	Family	Sex
Sex	Education	Career	Career
Career	Religion	Health	Health
Health	Community	Sex	Family
Friends	Career	Education	Friends
Education	Entertainment	Community	Sports

As is immediately apparent, Couple A's value assessment exhibits some marked differences. She sees her husband as being concerned with himself—Sex, Career, and Health come first for him in her opinion.

If he does value Family as highly as he says he does, how can his wife's perception be so low? She reports that Education is relatively unimportant on her list; yet he sees her as placing a high value on it. Could she be in school and he be feeling neglected? He values Friends and she recognizes that, but Friends is completely absent from her list and her husband's perception of what her list might include. Is she "busy and isolated" and possibly feeling that he does not give her much support? These are a few of the guesses that can be generated from lists like these. Progress can be assessed by charting any changes or perceived changes in lists.

Pew and Pew (1972) employ a similar technique. They ask each partner, in the other's presence, to rate himself or herself in seven areas:

1. Occupation
2. Love and marriage
3. Friendship
4. Getting along with self

5. Finding meaning in life
6. Leisure and recreation
7. Parenting

The first three are Adler's three life tasks (Adler, 1956; Dreikurs & Mosak, 1966); the next two are those added by Dreikurs and Mosak (Dreikurs & Mosak, 1967; Mosak & Dreikurs, 1967).

After the couples rate themselves, they are asked how they think their spouse would rate them, and then we elicit how the other actually rated them. Therapist and client can then discuss the perceptions (ratings) that each partner has of the other and how each feels about those perceptions. Therapeutic effort can then be directed to correcting those perceptions or modifying behaviors, should the couple so desire.

5

Confrontation Tactics

Shulman (1964/1973) defines confrontation as "any reasonable therapeutic technique which brings the client face to face with an issue in a manner calculated to provoke an immediate response" (p. 197). It has an element of challenge in it that is intended to forcefully make the client aware of choices. Confrontation does not always imply aggressiveness on the part of the therapist. It is not as the late Jackie Gleason, portraying Ralph Kramden in *The Honeymooners*, used to threaten, "Pow, right in the kisser!" In fact, many confrontations can be surgically subtle, even gentle, and still carry considerable impact. Shulman (1964/1973) makes a distinction regarding confrontations: those that are directed to the client's inner state (subjective feelings, beliefs/attitudes, and goals) and those that are directed to the client's overt behavior (what is being done, presenting alternatives, examining the future). Some confrontation tactics are discussed in the following pages.

WHEN?

For Adlerians, movement—not intentions—is the key to therapeutic success (see Chapter 3, "Conflict Resolution Tactics," and the Adlerian definition of insight on p. 20). Hillel (Hertz, 1958, 1:14), was accustomed to saying, "And if not now, when?" and we follow suit. Confronting a client with "when" she or he is going to change can be a powerful technique. "You say that you're going to change. When?" "When do you plan on starting?" "Why not right now?" Questions of this type require an immediate response and a commitment to change—or at least an acknowledgment on the part of the client that change is what is needed, not just "talk."

Mosak and Gushurst (1971) have discussed the difference between what patients say and what they mean, requiring us to "translate English into English." Such insights are very helpful in understanding some of the responses psychotherapists receive to the "when?" confrontation. "I should..." is a statement of intention the person does not intend to act upon. "I should stop washing my hands so much," the obsessive-compulsive says. This response basically means, "I should...but I'm not gonna." "I'll try" is a similar statement. The other half of the sentence is the implied, "but I don't expect to succeed."

Again, confrontation does not always mean "hitting the client between the eyes," so to speak. If the therapist sees confrontation in that manner, he or she may feel unable to confront. "When?" can be asked rather gently, yet emphatically. The issue is to "provoke an immediate response" (Shulman, 1973, p. 197).

CONFRONTING IMMEDIATE BEHAVIOR

"What are you doing right now?" Such a statement is intended to make the patient aware of what she or he is doing at the moment. Discrepancies between spoken and unspoken behavior are presented for examination. Often the client is not aware of such discrepancies. For example, we point out nonconscious body language. Given an interpretation, patients may appear superficially receptive and simultaneously be unconsciously "flicking" away the interpretation with their fingers. If they did realize what they are doing, many times they would not do it subsequently. For example, "You seem to be picking a fight with me. Is that your intention?"

An eight-year-old girl was seen in family therapy because she displayed a horizontal head tic that many therapists had unsuccessfully treated. The family was one in which every member was "gooder" than everyone else. The girl recognized her goal of being a good girl, but she also recognized an underlying rebellion against always having to conform. The therapist inquired, "Is it possible that on those occasions your mouth says, 'Yes,' and your head [here the therapist performed the tic] says, 'No!'?" Eight months later the tic had not returned.

RELATING THE PATIENT'S BEHAVIOR WITH THE THERAPIST'S

This technique is akin to confronting with immediate behavior, but the added dimension involves the therapist's use of his or her feelings and/or reactions. "You're picking a fight with me now. Is that what you want to do?" presents the client's behavior for examination, the added component being the therapist's re-action (in classical analytic jargon, countertransference reaction, as well). "I find myself frustrated and challenged. Is that what you're trying to elicit in me?" "I feel rather confused. Is that your intention?" "You're very funny. Are you trying to charm me or get me off the track?"

Along a similar vein, clients may "set up" the therapist for certain tactics of their own. A client who asks ("innocently," of course), "Am I boring you?" can be challenged with "Is that your intention?" In other instances, picking up on the therapist's tension, the patient may inquire, "Are you frustrated with me?"; the reply can be, "Do you want me to be? What would be the payoff or purpose?" The point is not to deny feelings that may be obvious, and therefore be what the communications analysts label "incongruent" (Haley, 1963), but rather to deal with the reality of the situation without becoming enmeshed in the patient's game.

POINTING OUT ALTERNATIVES

This involves confronting with alternatives, with the choices available to the clients (Mosak & Shulman, 1974). Typically, they develop "tunnel vision" with regard to lifestyle issues—that is, issues that are central, basic aspects of their lives. As a result of these blind spots, clients do not see alternatives open to them.

To illustrate, a client presented a problem relating to his job(s). He was quite capable and was usually given much responsibility—initially. Within a relatively short period of time, he found himself getting in "mixes" with his bosses and, sometime afterward, "fired." For this client there were only two methods of dealing with life and people. Either you stood up for what was "right" (and he knew better than anybody what that was) or you turned tail and ran away, an act that made one a "wimp." He was extremely intelligent and found himself in frequent confrontations with those above him, especially on issues in which he knew he was "right." Then he could become very sharp and sarcastic, efficiently so. He felt that if he "bit his tongue" and kept quiet, he was backing down and letting others walk all over him. For him, pointing out alternatives entailed exploring not only alternative responses to others but alternative explanations of their behavior. "What other comment might you make?" "What could be another way of doing that?" "What other reason could he have for saying that?" Those therapists who do role-playing may choose it as the vehicle.

Without the same lifestyle convictions of the client, the therapist can view problems from a broader, more commonsense vantage point. The therapist can point out or help the client discover alternative choices and options.

POINTING OUT BODY LANGUAGE

Confronting clients with their body language permits another means for provoking an immediate response. Fast (1970), Nierenberg and Calero (1971), and Guthrie (1977) present helpful guides to an understanding of body language. While confronting immediate behavior entails *what* a client is doing at the moment, pointing out body language adds the dimension of *how* the body is behaving during the process.

"You're grinding your teeth. What do you suppose that means?" "Every time I mention your father, you tense up and you pull back. Do you suppose that is saying something?" Or in a related style, "You tell me that I'm right and that you feel better talking about this, but your hands are wringing, and you're sweating quite a bit. Which is it? Do you feel better or are you actually anxious but just aiming to please me?"

Adler's *caveat* about trusting only movement is relevant here again. Faced with incongruent information, trust the body language. "It seems to me that there's a tear in your eye. While you maintain it doesn't bother you, I suspect it does."

BEING PERSISTENT

Some counselors tend to shy away from persistence because they believe it interferes with the client's freedom. Other counselors do not have this inhibition. As a student once described it, "Psychotherapy is the art of creative nagging." The persistence need not be hard, cold, and unfeeling. However, in order to persist, the therapist needs a good memory to keep the client on track.

On the other hand, persistence need not be limited to following a single train of thought. Rather it can be conceptualized as goal-directedness on the part of the therapist. If the client is viewed holistically, then what often appears as contradictory data can be reconciled with a clear understanding of the individual's style of living, by understanding the client's goals and movement in a broader context. Persistence can be applied to following the broader context, the overall pattern of the person's style of life. Someone whose goal is to be superior in all things can be consistently confronted with the goal in many areas of life. Dreikurs (Mosak & Shulman, 1974) referred to this as "monolithic interpretation."

Persistence also implies knowing the limits and strengths of the particular clients involved. Clients will respond both verbally and nonverbally, with cues that will signal when "enough is enough." Perseverance is one thing; badgering or fighting with the clients is another. It is the counselor's responsibility to be therapeutic, and that means dealing with the issues and topics that possess relevance to the process of change. The counselor may have to be persistent in his or her pursuit of topics and issues that clients need to face in order to change. While the counselor should not be in charge of the client, he or she should be in charge of the process. An old proverb reads, "Failure is the path of least persistence."

On a concrete level, an example of being persistent is the therapist who insists that a client discuss a troublesome topic. "Come on now, I know you're upset. Why don't you talk about it?" Reasons for the client's reluctance can be explored, along with possible fears/expectations of the consequences if the material should be "brought into the light of the day." On another level, an example of being persistent on an overall theme in contrast to a specific topic might be "Does this sound familiar to you? It does to me. It's your role of victim again. It seems you keep replaying it in different ways with different people."

One way of conceptualizing psychotherapy is to view it as bringing order to clients' lives, giving them the chance to recognize the recurrent patterns and themes (the script, the game, the lifestyle, the repetition compulsion), and then helping them to make healthier, more cooperative, socially useful, and self-fulfilling choices. Psychotherapists may have to be very persistent in order to make the patterns clear. And to repeat, it is requisite for the persistent therapist to possess a good memory.

Persistence also involves not permitting your patient to discourage you. Therapists, in spite of therapeutic difficulties, must retain their optimism. Instead of dwelling upon "I don't know what to do," which may lead to therapists' feeling discouraged and berating of self, they can also see this as a challenge to engage in problem solving. In the first instance, therapists become self-absorbed and withdraw their attention from the patient; in the second, they can devote themselves to the patient's problems rather than to their own.

6

Motivational Tactics

This chapter presents a group of tactics geared to help therapists increase clients' motivation to engage in therapy, to follow through with tasks, and in general, to take a more active stance in achieving therapeutically useful goals. The distinction between motivational deficit and educational deficit, however, needs to be made more explicit. More often than not, even among experienced clinicians, the two concepts are confused, and motivation is an issue that needs to be addressed throughout therapy, not just merely at the beginning.

Bandura (1977) has conducted research on the role of observational learning in human development. For years it was assumed that, in order to learn a particular behavior, reinforcement was required. If Johnny was to learn how to read, there had to be tangible rewards and reinforcement available in order for the process to work. What Bandura and his colleagues have demonstrated is that learning per se does not require reinforcement. An individual may acquire—that is, learn—a behavior through observation; reinforcement only encourages the use of that behavior. Johnny may know how to read; he simply may not have any motivation to demonstrate his skills. On a more commonsense level, many parents claim that they have shown their children "a hundred times" how to perform a task, to no avail. When parents are not about, they may do the task well; whenever the parents are around, the children "lose their ability" to do the task.

Psychotherapists must be aware of the above phenomenon. Many clients have problems as a result of poor early training. With some education (e.g., social skills training) they may do fine. Some, regardless of the amount of training, still do not seem to learn. This may not be a problem of learning; it may be one of lack of motivation to apply the learning.

"SELLING" PATIENTS WHAT THEY WANT

If a man enters a store looking for a red tie, the salesperson will have a difficult time selling him a pair of brown pants instead. Similarly, if a client enters therapy seeking assistance for one sort of problem, the therapist will encounter difficulty persuading the client that the problem is something else. If the man wanting the red tie is helped with that, his attitude toward the salesperson will be more receptive. For the salesperson to sell him the brown pair of pants, she or he has to show the customer how the two items are related ("A brown pair of pants would nicely highlight that new tie"). Because the salesperson has first sold him what he wants, the customer may be receptive to the salesperson's selling him something else, perhaps even brown pants. Clients approach therapy with their own agendas, and compliance with the therapeutic process can be greatly enhanced if the client feels he or she is getting what he or she came to "buy."

Life insurance salespeople acknowledge the value of this tactic. Years ago, the agent would attempt to persuade potential customers by attempting to impress them with the necessity for insurance, the value of insurance, and the low cost of insurance. The customer would very often reply, "I'll think about it" or "Even so, I can't afford it." Today, the agent asks the potential client, "What would you like to see happen to protect your family, to educate your children, to provide for your old age?" After the client has stated his wished-for objective, the agent replies, "I just happen to have a policy that will meet those objectives nicely and give you peace of mind."

Confronting adolescents with their poor self-images may be technically accurate but therapeutically inappropriate. Working on ways they can be more appealing to the other sex may produce greater motivation on their part. A young, chronic schizophrenic at a psychiatric day treatment center approached his therapist with a problem. He was always running out of money at the end of the month and being forced to borrow—and occasionally steal—money from others. In the past, this client had refused attempts to help him stick to a monthly budget. Rather than appeal to issues of control, ego strength, self-discipline, or ambivalence, the situation was presented to the client in the following manner. "You claim to feel bad when you run out of cigarettes the last week of every month. I can help make sure you never run out of cigarettes." This is what the client wanted to hear. The problem was presented to him in terms he would understand and focused on an issue that had meaning to him. Budgeting money for the sake of building self-discipline was meaningless to him; sticking to a budget so that he could buy cigarettes each week "hit home." Now he was motivated.

Teaching a husband good communications skills to improve the quality of the marriage takes on more significance if it is presented in a language he understands, according to goals that are relevant to him. "You say you don't have enough intimacy in the marriage. Perhaps if you displayed more empathy and showed your wife you cared more, let's say by utilizing some of these communication skills, she might be more receptive to you in general. She might want to feel closer to you. That could be the start of intimacy."

In general, motivation implies movement, and clients are constantly moving toward subjectively perceived and created goals. If the psychotherapist can use these goals in formulating treatment plans, client compliance will be greatly enhanced, as will client motivation.

THE USE OF PSYCHOLOGICAL TESTING

Mosak and Gushurst (1972) have discussed the therapeutic applications of psychological testing. From a motivational perspective, objective, computer-scored tests such as the Minnesota Multiphasic Personality Inventory-2 (MMPI-2) or the Millon

Multiaxial Inventory-III (MCMI-III) can be used to motivate hesitant, reluctant clients into engaging in therapy. For example, a young man who was referred for therapy by his mother felt that it was his mother, not he, who should be in therapy. The therapist made this offer: "I'd like to give you this test. You fill it in. Here's an envelope. On your way out throw it in the mailbox. It will go to a computer firm. The computer doesn't know you, it doesn't know your mother, and it doesn't care whether you're in therapy or not. In a few days we'll get the results back. If the results indicate that you need help for something, I'd like your commitment that you'll accept those results. If the results indicate that you don't need help for anything, I'll tell your mother to get off your back and stop nagging you." No adolescent has yet rejected this offer. Patients regard the test procedure as fair, and the therapist is not seen as an agent of the parent or whomever. They regard the procedure as "scientific," or "objective," and the fact the test is "untouched by human hands"—that is, not scored by the therapist—as a "fair" way of dealing with them. Unlike with the Rorschach or Thematic Apperception Test (TAT), which are hand scored and interpreted, therapist bias becomes a nonissue. The computer is impartial.

Intelligence tests can be used motivationally as well. Clients who feel they are "dumb" or "slow" can be given an intelligence test and "shown" their scores. A depressed, paranoid client, who repeatedly acted helpless and presented herself as unable to grasp simple conversations, was given a Wechsler Adult Intelligence Scale-Revised (WAIS-R). Her verbal score was 124, in the superior range. She was surprised, and her motivation to stop acting so confused and helpless was greatly improved.

Testing can be used to motivate patients to continue "working hard" in therapy. Changes in scores on tests (either the same taken twice or similar tests taken months apart) can serve to point out what has been accomplished and what yet has to be dealt with. Whether the tests employed are objective or subjective, patients tend to regard them as "objective," likening them to X rays or blood tests that can show "actual improvement."

Testing can also motivate clients to work on issues they once felt were hopeless. "I'm crazy—I must be losing my mind" is difficult to work on. Showing a client that she or he is not "crazy" or psychotic but rather simply experiencing anxiety over certain issues can facilitate her or his working on these particular issues. Raimy (1975) offers an illuminating view of the *strategies* for treating "phrenophobic" clients, that is those who fear they are "going crazy."

Projective tests, such as the TAT, Early Recollections [which Munroe (1955) considered to be the first projective test], or the Rorschach can be especially intriguing for the patient. Via the reports of such testing, the therapist can initiate many fruitful discussions. "How could you have known that?" or "What made you see that?" are signs that the client is at least curious, and therefore, for the moment, willing to discuss certain topics.

PLAYING "HARD TO GET"

Occasionally, clients will enter therapy reluctantly and make such statements as "I don't want to be here. I don't want help. I don't need help. And even if I did, I don't know whether I would want it from you." Rather than argue, persuade, or counter with "Okay, good-bye," one psychotherapist replied, "Wait a minute. The real question is whether I'm willing to choose you as a client. I'm a busy therapist and I don't take everyone who wants to see me. I take only those who really want my services, and I don't know that it would be you even if you did want my services. Give me three good reasons why I should consider taking you on as a client." Surprisingly enough, that which was unattractive five minutes before suddenly became attractive. Clients almost always give three reasons. The therapist may accept them (and the client) or may make the prospective client work harder. "Not good enough. I've heard all of those before. If you really want to be in therapy with me, you have to come up with some real compelling reasons." They usually do, and then the therapist can say, "All right, if you feel you want it that badly, I think I am willing to work with you."

Much of the same tactic can be used during the middle and final phases of therapy. Clients may be unwilling to raise or discuss issues that need to be discussed, and the therapist can play "hard to get" there as well. "I don't know if I really want to talk about that. I don't think there's much here to work with." The client response: "Well, if you knew what happened...."

THE "STICK"

The name of this technique comes from an old joke.

> A farmer coming down the road sees another farmer trying to get his balky mule to move. The owner of the mule pushes and pulls to no avail. The second farmer volunteers help that the first readily accepts. The second gets a large stick and begins to beat the mule. "Hold it," protests the first, "I don't want you to kill my mule. I just want you to get him moving." "That is exactly my intent, to get him moving, but first I have to get his attention."

Basically this tactic means, "better do it or else." "If this isn't settled, your wife is going to leave you." "Look, we either work on this or you won't be able to sleep for the next three months, either." "If we don't discover some way of dealing with your hallucinations, your family is going to put you back in the hospital."

Though not to be used very often, when it is used (in which case it will prove more effective), the "stick" tactic should be used so as to take advantage of the natural or logical consequences of the situation (Dreikurs & Grey, 1968; Dreikurs & Soltz, 1964). "If you keep sleeping late, you're going to get fired" places the burden on the client's shoulders and on the client's employer, not the therapist. The therapist is portrayed as someone who can help solve the problem, not enforce the solution.

GODFATHER TACTICS

Similar to the "stick" but more drastic are the Godfather tactics, offers that the patient cannot refuse. Asked to produce an early recollection during couples therapy, a man steadfastly maintained that he could not offer a single recollection before age 15, despite the therapist's urging. Suspecting that the patient's "I can't" meant "I won't," the therapist informed him, "I've never encountered anyone who wasn't brain damaged who couldn't give at least one early recollection." Offered the choice between possibly being brain damaged and relating early recollections, he chose the latter course. The therapist discussed with him why he pretended inability and was told that he, the patient, was there only "because my wife made me come." This issue was then dealt with so that therapy could resume.

THE "CARROT"

In another approach, the exhortation is "try it; you'll like it." Allowing the client to experience the positive rewards of certain behaviors/attitudes can be a powerful motivator. "If you are nicer to your wife, and we've discussed what nicer means, then you'll see just how much nicer she'll be to you." "Why don't you see what happens when you go to the party and do some of the things we've discussed? I'll bet you find you have a better time than you thought possible." Wolpe's (1965) offering of hope to Mrs. Schmidt, available on audiotape, represents another form of carrot.

THE "FIRE"

As with the "stick," the "fire" motivates the client to avoid some unpleasant consequences that are about to occur due to the client's own actions or inaction. However, this time, "It's already an emergency." "You've had two bypass operations already, and your physician has told you that you're heading for a third unless you change some things in life." "You've been fired for oversleeping again. Now you have no way to pay your bills. Isn't it time we worked on some things?"

The therapist can assume a more directive, involved stance with this technique. "Things are getting to the point where even I won't be able to help you unless you start to get moving here." "It may be getting too late for me to do much good. It may be out of my hands soon." Used sparingly, the "fire" can serve to encourage clients to actively work on their issues in therapy. Ferenczi and Rank (1925) introduced time limits into psychoanalysis, and the method has been used in Rogerian and Adlerian research (Shlien,

Mosak, & Dreikurs, 1962). Some therapists utilize deadlines to "pressure" the clients, but they often discover that it places pressure on themselves also.

Sometimes life itself creates the "fire," for example, the "driver" who says she can't slow down and then has a heart attack. She suddenly realizes that she can slow down.

"DO IT FOR ME"

With this tactic, the relationship between the client and the therapist is used to motivate the client to attempt something. "I know you're afraid, and that you'd rather not do this, but give it a shot, for me." The client is asked to do something for the therapist who, in turn, is asking the client to do something for himself. That is the crucial aspect to this tactic. Though the client may be doing it for the therapist, in reality, it is for the client's own good. "Just one time, go out with a woman after work just for 15 minutes. Do it for me!" If the therapeutic relationship is solid, this can prove very potent.*

The therapist should bear in mind Dreikurs and Soltz's (1964) admonition about "mother deafness." Used too frequently, the therapist's requests may be tuned out by the client. For this tactic to be rendered effective, it should be used rarely with clients; moreover, there are several possible pitfalls. The patient may blame the therapist if the task "backfires" and accuse, "Look what you got me in to" or may feel that, having done something for the therapist, now it's the therapist's turn to do something for him or her. The careful clinician will avoid these situations.

"FOR AN EXTRA QUARTER YOU CAN SEE WHAT'S INSIDE"

This tactic is designed to intrigue clients, to take advantage of their curiosity. Setting up situations that "tease" the client in an in-

---

*It may also be used in the following way. "Why should I do it for father (mother, etc.)?" "OK, don't do it for them. Do it for me."

triguing, motivating way may make the client receptive. "I know that you're upset about that argument with your boss. If you'd be willing to work with me on it, I think I could show you some fascinating things about how you interact with people." "It seems to me that you're curious about what happened with your friend last night. Maybe you'd be willing to find out how that can happen every night." "You seem interested in learning about how you operate. You might see things about yourself you never dreamed of."

A hospitalized, depressed patient refused to cooperate in treatment because "I can't be cured." She remained in bed, with the intention of remaining there until her insurance ran out and she would be transferred to a state hospital, where she planned to spend the remainder of her life. A new therapist refuted her notion that depression could not be cured, a statement that came as a surprise to her, and challenged her with, "If you want to start on the curing process, be in the day room fully dressed tomorrow at 9 A.M., and we'll start." The following morning she arrived in the day room completely dressed, but at 9:10. She was told, "Apparently you are not yet sufficiently motivated to start the curative process. If you *really* want to get rid of your depression, be here tomorrow by 9." She was.*

The bottom line of this technique is to motivate the client to work meaningfully in therapy. If one captures the client's attention, if one can make the task appear worth looking at, then the client will be more motivated to "take a look inside."

USING THE PATIENT'S OWN INCENTIVE

When children experience difficulty in school, teachers attempt direct remedial measures that often fail. Others take another route. If the child presents a reading difficulty, they locate an interest of the child—for example, baseball. They leave baseball books around, relying on the child's incentive to pick up a book to see what's inside. Then the child may ask to learn to read better in order to understand the content of the book. We refer to this as

---

*This tactic is often used in drug clinics.

"the golden bridge." The same process can be used in psychotherapy.

A schizophrenic woman was in the midst of her sixth hospitalization. On the previous hospitalizations, she had been treated with medication and shock treatment. Now she literally fought against any treatment interventions because "they [the staff] might kill me." A consultant was invited to interview her to attempt to obtain her consent to treatment. She indicated to the consultant that the staff might wish to kill her "because I have a special relationship with God." She then narrated three instances in which she had met God, each time in a bar. "Imagine! God seeking *me* out for a drink." In the first instance, after a few drinks, "God" invited her to go to bed with him at a motel. "Imagine! Of all the women in the world, God picked *me*!" After this afternoon seance, she went home to cook dinner. When her husband arrived home, her husband, detecting her cheerfulness, made inquiries, and she related the afternoon's events. He exploded with rage and proclaimed, "I'll kill you!" After she related the two other encounters with "God," the consultant agreed, "It seems you really do have a special relationship with God." The patient responded, "You know, every time I've prayed to God, God has answered my prayers." "Every time?" "Every time." "I'm glad to learn that, because when we're through, why don't you go back to your room and pray to God not to let anyone harm you?" She does not tarry. She begins to pray right there. The tension oozes out of her. She is now *perfectly safe.*

7

Paradoxical Tactics

Mozdzierz, Macchitelli, and Lisiecki (1976) have presented a detailed, useful review of the use of paradox in psychotherapy, particularly in relation to Adlerian theory and technique. Adler (1927) is generally considered the first to have used paradoxical intention clinically,* though he referred to it as "negative suggestion" (Adler, 1956, p. 346). Wexberg (1929/1970), another Adlerian, used the term "antisuggestion." Both terms were confused with the proposal of suggestive therapeutics and later were dropped. Frankl (1967, 1985), who worked with Adler prior to the former's internment in a concentration camp, eliminated the confusion by renaming the technique as "paradoxical intention." For a comprehensive overview of the tactic itself, Weeks and L'Abate (1982), Omer (1981), and Ascher (1989) present an in-depth analysis of paradoxical treatments from different perspectives.

For present purposes, paradoxical tactics are of two types: (a) inviting the client to do the opposite of what is anticipated or "normal," and (b) the psychotherapist's doing the opposite of what the client expects. In general, however, paradoxical tactics are effective in that they "decontextualize" the symptom (Omer, 1981, p. 322). In other words, "The modifications created in the symptoms context by the therapist transform this context in such

---

*Knight Dunlap (1933), a learning theorist, referred to this as the theory of "negative practice."

a manner that the symptom loses its function and meaning" (Omer, 1981, p. 322). In effect, the purpose of the symptom is lost. Frankl (1969) and Mosak (1987a) have also pointed out the role of humor in paradoxical intention.

ANTISUGGESTION AND PARADOXICAL INTENTION

A pretty, overweight young woman complained to her therapist about the "usual things," but made special effort to mention the fact that she "can't stay away from chocolate." The therapist inquired, "Is that all?" to which she replied, "If I could only stay away from chocolate, I would have no trouble losing weight." He took out his prescription pad and wrote down for her to "take" a certain number of ounces of chocolate six times a day. She looked at him and thought he was crazy. He said, "I'm your doctor and that's an official prescription." She got so sick of chocolate that just the mention of the word turned her stomach. In effect, chocolate was no longer useful—it had lost its purpose for her as a means of rewarding herself.

Another therapist used the paradoxical tactic with a young schizophrenic. The patient's pacing was disrupting to everyone, and all attempts to regulate or alter the behavior proved futile. This client frequently discontinued treatment at other centers by "running away" and hitchhiking across the country (note the emphasis upon movement). With the assistance of the other clients at the center, the client was encouraged to continue pacing, but this time, with other clients. Whenever he felt like pacing, the client was instructed to do so, but henceforth it would be *with* other clients or a staff person who would use the opportunity to socialize with him. He stopped pacing; the purpose of the symptom was defeated—he could no longer isolate himself through his pacing. To pace now became equated with socializing.

NOT FIGHTING THE SYMPTOM

When one experiences a symptom, there is a natural tendency to fight it. After all, why should the person continue to suffer? What is little understood is that, by fighting the symptom, one not only maintains it but may even escalate it. Take stage fright (Horvat, 1937), for example. If to reduce anxiety, one tells oneself, "I mustn't be nervous," one focuses on the "nervousness," reinforces it, and perhaps makes it worse. An analogy will help. Suppose you are seasick. "It" wants to come up, and you want to keep "it" down. Having swallowed "it" down, "it" now requires even greater force than initially, and then it requires even greater force to push "it" down. Pretty soon you are so sick you don't care whether you live or die. This was a lesson learned during World War II, when it took weeks to evacuate casualties to the United States. During those weeks these military personnel had ample opportunity to fight their symptoms. Today, we teach patients not to fight their symptoms. Some therapists advocate practicing (actually deliberately "rehearsing") the symptoms.

WRITING DOWN THE SYMPTOMS

For clients who have an inordinate number of complaints—for example, somatizers or hypochondriacs—when they are asked to write down their symptoms each time they have them, it becomes a burdensome task. For example, with a hypochondriac, the therapist may say, "I am willing to help you if you give me some information. What I would like you to do is keep a pad of paper and a pencil with you and every time you experience a symptom, please write down the symptom, the time of day it occurred, what you did about it, and whether or not what you did made it better or worse. When we meet next, we'll spend time talking about it and see if we can make some sense of it. Then maybe we can be in a position to see if we can make the symptoms go away." Almost always the client arrives at the next session without a list. "I wouldn't have time to do anything else if I did that list." At that point the issue can be turned back. "Apparently you didn't feel that your symptoms were important enough to do the prescribed task. Let's talk about something else, something other than your symptoms."

Discussion can then center on responsibility for self or about attention getting, as the case may be. What occurs is that the patient stops complaining about the symptoms and finally begins to talk about his or her attitudes, feelings, or motivation, or says that the task of writing down all the symptoms is more trouble than it is worth. Adler (1927, 1956) often prescribed this kind of "homework" for clients who complained of sleeplessness. He asked them to make a list of their thoughts at night, especially those that were keeping them awake, so they could discuss them the next day. Rarely, if ever, is the list presented, and the issue of sleeplessness is virtually always settled. The patient often falls asleep to avoid the prescribed task.

"WHEN DO WE COME TO THE BAD PART?"

The psychotherapist can do what is unexpected as well. Clients often present themselves as "terrible" people who have committed "horrible" transgressions, thus inviting the therapist to place himself or herself in the role of "garbage collector" (Mosak & Shulman, 1974). They bait the therapist: "What I've done is so terrible I can't even tell you about it," they say. The greater interest the therapist displays, the more resistant the client becomes. The therapist's response to such a game may be as simple as "OK, if you can't tell me, let's go on to something else." Typically their intention is to shock, to throw the therapist off balance, to pique the therapist's interest and invite a possible power contest, to impress the therapist with the gravity of their "sin," or to get the therapist to force them to tell what they could voluntarily tell.

When clients do "confess," it is usually no more than what others do or have done without feeling guilty about it. When they finish, the therapist sits silently and doesn't utter a word. They anticipate that the therapist will say something like "That's awful!" or "We'd better get to work on that immediately," or will even dismiss "blackguards" like themselves from therapy. But the therapist, to the patient's surprise, says nothing until finally the patient says, "Well, aren't you going to say something?" "Sure" is the reply, "right after we get to the bad part."

A variation of this can be employed with clients who are convinced that what they are doing is cause for concern and a sign of their "sickness." One bipolar client, currently in a paranoid-depressive phase, attempted to convince the staff and family alike with how "rotten" he was, how "bad" he had been, and that he should be punished for it. Despite several medication adjustments, the delusional quality and intensity persisted. Finally, the therapist offered a variation of the "When do we get to the bad part?" tactic. He commented that what the client was experiencing was a relief to hear, and that it was a good sign that the client was beginning to emerge from his depression. As a matter of fact, it was a healthy sign that the client was regaining his sense of "right and wrong" and that things were going along on schedule.* The client was caught off-guard, and the entire staff was urged to assume a similar stance to that of his therapist. His depressed, paranoid delusions halted by the next morning.

With the altering of the therapist's response to such behavior, the client is confronted with a new set of behaviors, which is not normally encountered in the client's world. One such role is that of "the crazy therapist," discussed by O'Connell (1975b) and Mosak (1987a). Generally, the client's symptoms are designed to elicit certain types of responses from others—and when these responses are not given, the client is forced to change behaviors. To use a tennis analogy, the therapist must not return the patient's serve to that part of the court where the patient is standing, anticipating the therapist's return.

"SPITTING IN THE CLIENT'S SOUP"

Adler (1956) coined this somewhat unpalatable, but memorable, phrase. In effect, if you "spit" in someone's soup, he or she may still choose to eat it, but it will no longer taste as good as it did initially. If the client understands the purpose of the symptom, for example, it may still be used, but it will lose much of its desired effect.

A mother came in crying to her therapist's office, claiming that she had ruined her child's life. "I've completely ruined my child," she wailed, expecting the therapist to disagree and an "argument" to ensue, with the therapist experiencing futility in any attempt to reassure or console her. Since many therapists believe

---

*Mosak and Shulman (1974) refer to this as "explaining the natural course of the dis-ease."

that children have choice, and that, in spite of what parents may do by way of childrearing, the child can still decide how he or she wants to turn out, the therapist quietly urged the mother to "quit bragging." It was explained to her that when a mother says she has completely ruined her child's life, she is portraying herself as the sole influence upon the child. The father, siblings, teachers, other children, the church all affect the child, although none of them is as "powerful" as she is. With this pointed out to her, she has the choice of continuing to "brag" or of examining her role in a more realistic way. She could not easily complain about that issue to the therapist again.

Another client, a young woman, often claimed she could do "supernatural things" such as read minds, prophesize from dreams, and so forth. She used this as a rationale for not socializing and not connecting with other people. They just weren't like her; they wouldn't understand. The therapist responded by interpreting to her that obviously she was a "special" person who wanted to be recognized as such. Every time she has these thoughts she was telling herself just how special she wanted to be. This interpretation invited her to examine her claims for specialness and superiority, and to examine them "publicly." She rapidly lost interest in the supernatural and stopped using that as an excuse for her avoidance of the social realm.

"Spitting in the soup" requires that the psychotherapist understand the purpose of the symptom in relation to the patient's social field (Shulman & Mosak, 1967). Adler (1956) was fond of quoting Socrates, who reportedly said to a young man who walked around the streets of Athens in a worn and tattered garb, "Your vanity peeps through the holes in your robe... (p. 232)." The therapist needs to be aware of such contradictions and to realize that the contradictions are probably only "apparent." In reality, the client is looking to gain something from the symptoms. Making that "public," that is, exposing it to the light of common sense, deflates the purpose.

This tactic is not restricted to the eradication of symptoms but can be directed toward attacking some lifestyle convictions (Shulman & Mosak, 1988) or what Ellis and Harper (1975) refer to as "irrational beliefs." A therapist treating a college English major discovered that his client interpreted everything in terms of masculinity, and that many of his behaviors made him either more or less masculine. He demanded of himself that he be the "realest" of real men and was in fights with other men regularly. For a long time he did not date for fear that the woman might discover that he was not a "real man." Eventually he arrived at the point at which he would date, but he started playing a game. He would take his date to a bar or restaurant and, sometime during the evening, would turn to a man sitting nearby and threaten, "I don't like the way you're looking at my girl." The men usually picked themselves up and sat elsewhere, figuring "Who needs this?" This, he assumed, impressed his date with his masculinity.* As he and his therapist conversed, he constantly boasted of his masculine exploits. One day, in response to such a boast, the therapist exclaimed, "You really are a vain guy." Huffily the client demanded, "So what's wrong with that? I have something to be vain about." To which the therapist responded, "As an English major you should know that 'Vanity, thy name is woman.'"

Kurt Adler (1961) illustrates how he uses this tactic with some suicidal patients.

> Patients have tested me with the question, how I would feel if I were to read of their suicide in the newspaper. I answer that it is possible that some reporter hungry for news would pick up such an item from a police blotter. But, the next day, the paper will be old, and only a dog perhaps may honor the suicide notice by lifting a leg over it in some corner. (p. 66)

THE TEN-FINGER TACTIC

A commonly encountered phenomenon is the "low self-esteem" problem. Patients flagellate themselves with "I'm a failure," "I never do anything right," "I don't like (respect) myself," and similar phrases. When patients embark on this path, one way of in-

---

*He was eventually "cured" of this behavior, not by his therapist, but by a man who put a gun to the patient's head, and challenged, "And what do you want to do about it?"

terrupting their self-depreciation is to ask them to list ten nice, positive things about themselves. After some jousting back and forth, they usually come up with two or three traits. "Isn't that enough? I just can't come up with any more." Holding up three fingers, the therapist indicates, "You still have seven to go," and then waits in silence. This has two effects on clients. First, it provides them with an awareness of how they usually focus their attention upon the negative rather than the positive. Second, it shows the therapist's faith in the fact there is something good about them. The list making can be altered to fit the situation, such as listing ten nice things about your children or ten nice things that happened to you this week or month. Since both good and bad things occur to everyone, what is attended to becomes a matter of choice. Which will the client attend to most?

When clients have laboriously completed the task, they breathe a sigh of relief. The therapist may then inquire, "Supposing I told you I knew a person who..." and repeats the ten traits the client named, "What would you say about such a person?" Some clients will observe that she or he would be a "nice person"; others will reply with a smile, "I'd like to meet him or her." The therapist can then offer to make an introduction. Or the therapist can carry this a bit further by requesting the client to obtain a small pocket calendar in which to record daily one nice, positive thing he or she is, has done, or will do. Clients usually acquiesce, and the therapist informs them that since this is a hazardous experiment, informed consent is required. As the patient looks puzzled, the therapist explains, "At the end of one year you will have 365 entries in your calendar. How will you then maintain the myth that you're a failure (rotten, inferior, unworthy, etc.)?"

This tactic can also be used in a variation in marital therapy. Many couples seek marital therapy in order to complain about each other. In such sessions each is asked to say ten positive things about the partner. If they cannot, there is probably little hope for the marriage. If they can, it can change the atmosphere of the sessions and the attitudes of the couple. Not only are there problems to be "solved," but strengths upon which to build. Both would be the focus of the therapeutic work rather than the fault finding that often characterizes marital therapy sessions.

In situations in which the clients expect the therapist to dwell upon the negative solely, such a paradoxical request can be very useful. It is not the therapist who is coming up with the list of positives (as many in the clients' social world do), it is the clients themselves. Should the couple, for instance, be unable or unwilling to comply, the therapist can respond with "If there's nothing nice about him (or her), you're one poor judge of character. Why would you marry someone who has nothing nice about him (or her)?" Rather than a gripe session, the emphasis changes to a more realistic one; while negative issues may still exist and must be dealt with, everybody experiences such issues. A more workable perspective is introduced in that one can explain to one's clients that it is very difficult to be served in a restaurant if one tells the waiter only what one does *not* want. People do not get very far with that approach. In order to get one's needs met, eventually a commitment has to be made to what *is* wanted, and then movement can be made toward that. By listing the positive, movement is initiated toward what is wanted. Corsini (1967) has devised a "first aid kit for marriage" in which he invites spouses to tell what they want and move toward it.

FOCUSING ON THE POSITIVE

While many patients acknowledge a self-esteem problem, they do not know how to elevate their self-esteem. They feel that they have to change themselves over completely. The therapist counters this idea.

> In everyone's head there are ideas, convictions, and memories which are both positive and negative. If one focuses on the positive, one will come to the conclusion that one is OK. If one, on the other hand, focuses on the negative ideas, one will conclude that one is not OK. So it is not a matter of changing yourself so much as changing what ideas you choose to focus on, the positive or the negative. It makes more sense, even if we acknowledge our defeats and our deficiencies, to focus on the positive because first, you'll feel better and second, people who believe that they're OK generally function better in life.

GIVING UP

Manaster and Corsini (1982) make a distinction between two forms of this tactic, an approach that should be used sparingly.* The therapist may "give up" or urge the client to give up. Adler (1956) discussed the depreciation tendency in clients, a tendency they may use both in and out of therapy. In therapy, the tendency of these clients is to first elevate the therapist and then knock down the therapist, to degrade the therapist or his or her skills. By building up the therapist, the clients place themselves in position to defeat the therapist and avoid the therapeutic task. Mosak and Gushurst (1971) offer an illustration of how the therapist's succumbing to client flattery may turn the former into a pawn of the latter. "Giving up" can be unexpected and throw clients off balance, thus disrupting their game.

In the initial form of this tactic (Manaster & Corsini, 1982), the psychotherapist simply admits defeat and places responsibility back on the client. "We've worked on this many times and yet you still continue to do it. I give up. I guess I can't help you with it." By admitting that the client is "tougher" and that the therapist is "powerless"—not "weak"—in this situation, the client's game is spoiled. The victory is less sweet. Many times the client then assumes the responsibility for working on the issue. "Well, it's really not that bad, you know. Maybe if...."

Another variation on this theme is to ask the client to give up. The therapist says, "You're right; that is pretty tough. Maybe you should just give up and accept that fact that things won't change." The "power struggle" is deflated and the client's sense of control is shaken. The therapist may continue, "I guess you'll never be able to confront him. You can learn to live with it." Some therapists resort to quoting the second line of the serenity prayer[†] at this point. The client often responds with "There's gotta be something I can do." If the client is playing Berne's (1964) game of "Why don't you—Yes but,"[‡] the roles can now be reversed

---

*A form of this technique may be used in marriage counseling (Phillips & Corsini, 1982).

[†]The prayer, used by Alcoholics Anonymous, is often attributed to St. Francis of Assisi and Reinhold Niebuhr: "God grant me the courage to change the things I can, the serenity to accept the things I cannot change, and the wisdom to know the difference."

[‡]Adler (1956) introduced this phrase to describe the movement of the neurotic.

(O'Connell & Brewer, 1971), with the client producing alternatives rather than the therapist doing so and the client shooting them down.

Urging the client to give up can also invite client resistance. The therapist may urge as follows:

> Therapy is a two-person game like tennis or chess. The games we usually play are what we call zero-sum games. That is, if you win, I lose. If I win, you lose. And the amount you win by is the amount I lose by. However, the therapy "game" is not a zero-sum game. It has different outcomes. In therapy, if I win, you win. If you win, you lose. How about throwing the game to me and letting me win?

WHAT WOULDN'T YOU CHANGE?

Coyne (1984) and the group at the Mental Research Institute of California have created a number of techniques for use in couples therapy but which may also be used in individual and family therapy.

Clients are asked, typically within the first few sessions, "What wouldn't you change about yourself (your marriage, your job, your family life, etc.)? I know it may be hard to think of right now, but obviously your perceptions may be a little off for the moment. If you were going to change, what would you want to keep the same because you are happy with it?" Such a question has a number of purposes. Like the ten-finger tactic, it focuses upon the positives in the client's lives. Second, it has a subtle implication that alters the mindset of many clients—they are going to change. They are in control of what they want to change and what they do not. Third, it creates a more positive therapeutic atmosphere. The therapist is taking for granted that, though clients may be having problems, they can and do have positive aspects about themselves. They can do some things right. And fourth, it can interrupt the litany of complaints that frequently are heard in the initial interviews so that therapeutic work can proceed.

8

Imagery Tactics

Clients are excellent at creating images and maintaining images that move them in useless, nonproductive ways. A young man creates an image of being laughed at and ridiculed when asking a girl for a date. A woman refuses to confront her boss because she can picture the way he will "shoot her down." A student hesitates speaking up in class because he is afraid he will give a "wrong, stupid" answer and can almost hear the class derisively whispering about how foolish he is. These are just a few of many examples we encounter with clients who have trained themselves in various safeguarding behaviors.

Symptoms require care and feeding (Mosak & Shulman, 1974); otherwise they tend to fade with time and lose their intensity. Creating images furnishes a way of reminding themselves and "nurturing" symptoms in the absence of avoided stimuli. Such images can be more overwhelming than the stimuli themselves.

This rich vein of material can be "mined," and the creative power of the individual can be redirected in more useful ways. A creative therapist will attempt to figure out what will move a patient, and once the patient is on the move, the creative therapist will keep the movement going. It has been jokingly said that Freud stayed "behind" his patients; Rogers stayed "with" his clients; and Adler stayed "one step ahead" of his. If that witticism possesses any element of truth, then using images can be a productive way of moving and staying one step ahead of clients.

"HANDLES"

Simply stated, we mentally give each person a name, and when it is appropriate, we divulge it to the person (Mosak, 1995). When the name is divulged and if it is accurate, the client will smile and respond with a recognition reflex (Dreikurs, 1967a) and/or a statement such as "That's me!" If done in a good-natured manner, in a manner intended to help but not harm the person (Mosak, 1995), the "handle" will be a good reminder to the client of what goals he or she is striving to attain.

Some therapists, notably transactional analysts (Steiner, 1974) ask the client to create the "handle," saying, for example, "If you had a sweatshirt and wanted to put a description of yourself across the chest, what one or two words would you place there?" Names such as "little princess," "tough guy," and "strong but silent" are one type of "handle." More specifically, "Lot's wife" can be used to refer to someone who is preoccupied with looking over her shoulder to the past. Such patients can be informed of a remark made by the philosopher-physician Maimonides (1982) that "Our eyes are set in the front and not in the back. One should therefore look ahead of him and not behind him" (p. 127). Dreikurs used the appellation "Mrs. God" to refer to those mothers who wanted always to be right or in control. "Jolting Joe" can be used for men who feel they have "to get the first punch in." Manaster and Corsini (1982) provide several examples of such names. "Dr. Doolittle" alludes to those who prefer animals to humans, and generally avoid people. "Mack the Knife" is on the lookout for enemies and is ready to take them by force. "Little Orphan Annie" is alone in a hostile world but goes on bravely, and naively (pp. 139–140). They, as well as Adler (1929/1964a) and Mosak (1995), provide additional examples.

Therapists need to be creative themselves. They have to be able to draw upon the patient's history and style to find (or create) an accurate "handle." Clients can use this name as a thumbnail reminder of both what they expect from life and others and how they go about "setting up" situations to fulfill these assumptions.

METAPHORS

Lenrow (1996), Gordon (1978), Angus and Rennie (1989), Mosak (1995), and Kopp (1995) have discussed the use of metaphor in psychotherapy. Lenrow delineates four functions that metaphors serve:

1. A willingness to explore novel thoughts about self and discard old assumptions and choices,
2. Increased attention to specific actions and transactions,
3. Recognition of the contribution of one's own style, especially in relation to others, and
4. A form of learning that is transferable to other settings. By metaphors, we mean "language referring to visual, auditory, or bodily events of a concrete sort" (Lenrow, 1966, p. 145). Examples would be images such as "You're dragging your feet" or "You feel smothered."

Other writers on the subject use broader definitions of metaphors. What metaphors provide is an awareness of "events," whereas "handles" usually refer to the subject (with the contextual emphasis implied). Metaphors are used here to establish more of a "concrete" relationship between subject and situation. In practice, a client can be confronted with a metaphor for the current predicament he or she is in. For instance, "You look like someone who's been through the wringer. How long are you going to let him (or her) put you through this?" If accurate, it can serve as a vivid reminder and motivator the next time the client is in the same situation. It can add a sense of validation and allow the client to quickly sum up and grasp a number of complex transactions, feelings, and thoughts and then more efficiently choose appropriate courses of action.

Metaphors can also be discovered in early recollections (Kopp, 1995; Mosak, 1995). A woman relates the following early memory:

"I lived on a farm. It was a super rainy day, and I was returning from school. I crossed the field. It was very muddy, and I sank to my waist in the mud, and I couldn't get out. I felt trapped." Independent of the interpretation of this recollection, we detect the metaphor of being "a stick in the mud."

A client confided in her therapist the effects a metaphor had upon her interactions with her ex-husband. "I was starting to argue with him on the phone," she said, "when I remembered what we'd talked about. I started getting that feeling again, you know, like I was trying to swim upstream against the current, and I stopped. I figured, 'What the hell—who needs this?' and I got out of it. My whole day wasn't ruined."

IMAGERY

Whereas "handles" refers to names highlighting personality styles and metaphors relate to the person-situation, images are symbols that clients are asked to generate to alter their behavior. Mosak (1995) provides an example of this tactic with a client who was having trouble with intercourse. In group therapy he was asked why dogs never seem to experience difficulty "doing it." He was instructed to think of that image the next time he attempted intercourse and say to himself, "Bow wow!" Upon his return to the group, he reported that he had successfully "bow wowed."

One therapist informs his self-aggrandizing and self-minimizing patients that they live life as if they were carrying around those distorting carnival mirrors that make people appear larger, smaller, or distorted.

Being very situation-specific, such images vary from client to client. A client who was accustomed to having things done her way was very challenged by anyone who threatened her power. She would set out to "take them down a notch or two." She was given the "handle" of "David" and told that the next time she went out "giant killing," she should look around for a slingshot. This image helped to interrupt the behavior.

CONCRETE IMAGES

Images are "concrete" in that they actually exist. Rather than simply imaging or symbolically performing an act, the client is given something "to carry around" that will serve as a reminder. Rebels can be given little Confederate flags. A second-born child who still feels the competitiveness with an older sibling and carries it into adult life can be given an "Avis—We try harder!" button. "Babies" can be given a bib to carry around with them. One therapist gave a tiny whip to a client to carry around in his pocket with which to beat himself up when needed. Such a tactic serves as a reminder to the client and as a concrete prompt.

Every statement one patient made was succeeded by the word "but." The therapist asked her to purchase an inexpensive dictionary but did not reveal why. His intent was to obliterate the word "but" with a marking pen and for her to keep the dictionary open on that page at home to remind her that the word no longer existed for her in the English language. When the therapist opened the dictionary to delete the word, he discovered to his own amazement and that of the patient that "but" had been omitted.

Some therapists distribute postcards* that can be very funny to clients. Some of them read:

"I challenge you to a friendship."
"All I want is a little more than I'll ever get."
"I am unconditionally guaranteed to be full of defects."
"Wait a minute. Come back. There's a part of my face you haven't stepped on yet!"

FUTURE AUTOBIOGRAPHY

The future autobiography is based upon a recurrent episode in John Steinbeck's *Of Mice and Men* (1937). George and Lenny are

---

*For more information about these products, write Brilliant Enterprises, P.O. Box 14285, San Francisco, CA 94114.

itinerant farmhands who "ride the rails" from place to place seeking employment. To while away the long hours in the boxcars, Lenny, who is mentally retarded, pleads,

> "Come on, George. Tell me. Please, George. Like you done before.... Go on now, George, you got it by heart."
> "You can do it yourself."
> "No, you. I forgot some a' the things. Tell about how it's gonna be."

George responds with a future autobiography. "Okay. Someday we're gonna get the jack together and we're gonna have a little house and a couple of acres an' a cow and some pigs...we'll have a big vegetable patch and a rabbit hutch and chickens. And when it rains in winter we'll just say the hell with going to work, and we'll build up a fire in the stove an' listen to the rain comin' down on the roof—Nuts! I ain't got time for no more" (pp. 28–30).

Mosak and Maniacci (1995) and Nikelly and O'Connell (1971) present examples and discuss the use of the future autobiography. The client is asked to describe himself or herself at some time in the future, five or ten years, for instance. One client reported that, in ten years, either he would be great, successful, and happy or he would be King of the Bums (an image), just wandering the streets with long hair, dirty, and with no one to care about him.* Asking clients to project into the future can prove very emotionally meaningful for them and an effective way to assess both goals —the willingness to work in therapy—and hope. The task can be varied. The client can be asked to imagine what life would be like if therapy were successful and if therapy were not, that is, if life does not change and present styles remain intact. The client can then be prompted with phrases such as "You're heading for that image of being alone, lonely, sitting in front of a small TV set, eating a stale, frozen dinner in a dingy room. Is that where you want to end up?" (The latter is a confrontation statement.)

---

*We observe here the *"aut Caesar aut nihil"* outlook of the cyclothymic personality and the bipolar disorder (Mosak & Shulman, 1966).

THE PUSHBUTTON TACTIC

Adler is considered by many to be one of the first cognitive psychotherapists (Bedrosian & Beck, 1980; Shulman, 1985). He believed that ideas, our opinions of "facts," influenced both our emotions and behavior. By changing one's opinions or ideas, one could change moods, a concept Beck (1976) has built upon in his cognitive treatment of depression. Mosak (1985, 1995) has also used this concept in working with depressed clients. He points out that a depressed client is discouraged, and in order for therapy to progress, it is advisable to interrupt the depression, thereby offering some encouragement to the client. The tactic is introduced this way:

> This is a three-part experiment. Please close your eyes and keep them closed until all three parts are over. First, I'd like you to dig into your memory and find a happy moment, a pleasant memory—a success, a time when you were loved, a beautiful sunset—and project it in front of your eyes as if you were watching it on TV. Watch it from beginning to end and relive the feeling you had at the time of the incident. Now begin. Remember how wonderful it was! When you are through, hold up a finger to signal that you are through, and we'll continue to the next part.

When the client signals that the "TV show" is over, we proceed to the second part.

> Now I'd like you to go back in your memory and find a horrible incident. You were sick; someone died; you were rejected; you failed. Watch it from beginning to end as if it were on TV and attach to it the feelings you had then. Go. Remember how terrible it was! Again, when you are through, hold up a finger and we'll proceed to Part Three.

When the signal is given, we conclude as follows:

> Now, go back and retrieve another pleasant memory, and if you can't find a second one, go back to the pleasant memory in Part One. Watch it "on TV" from beginning to end and relive the feel-

ings you had then. Remember how great it was, how wonderful! When you are through, please open your eyes.

When the "experiment" is finished, clients are asked to discuss it. We aim to help the client make the following associations:

1. What one feels depends on what one thinks.* If one thinks of pleasant material, one feels good; if one thinks of unpleasant material, one feels bad.
2. Instead of feeling that one is a victim of depression, that depression has one in its grip and won't let go, the client can observe that she or he creates the depression by what she or he thinks.
3. Instead of feeling helpless to control the depression, the client learns that she or he can control the depression. The client learns that she or he is responsible for creating and maintaining the depression (Shulman & Mosak, 1967). Since the client can maintain it, the client can also eliminate it.
4. It need not take "forever" to interrupt the depression. After all, the client can shift from an unpleasant feeling to a pleasant feeling in one moment.

When the client understands these concepts, the therapist informs the client that he or she will be taking home two imaginary pushbuttons—a "Happy" button and a "Depressed" button. If the client presses the "Happy" button, he or she will think pleasant thoughts and have pleasant feelings. If, on the other hand, the client returns to the next interview still feeling depressed, he or she will be asked why, in view of the fact the client could have pressed the "Happy" button, the depressed one was chosen. "In that case we'll have to discuss your investment in continuing to be depressed." This tactic helps interrupt depressions and restores in clients an internal locus of control, provides a sense of hope that they can do something about their "condition," and facilitates further examination of the depression. Brewer (1976) has found this a very effective procedure in treating

*More technically, underlying every feeling there is some cognition (Dreikurs, 1967a; Ellis & Harper, 1975). Thus, anger reflects the cognition, "There is something I feel needs changing."

situational depression. Fagan (1975) describes a similar technique for treating headaches.

STORIES

Fox (1980) discusses the role of stories in psychotherapy, noting that one function of being human is to invent stories. "It follows then that a purpose of therapy is to help patients to invent better ones...patients may be seen as suffering from stories which are inadequate to the needs of the world as experienced" (p. 40). Berne (1972) has talked about life "scripts" and draws the parallel to Adler's conception of the "lifestyle." Both see individuals as creating stories or "dramas" that are acted out in daily life. Fox elaborates upon the use of stories in therapy. He tells stories to clients and has them tell stories back, with communication occurring at many levels (literally, symbolically). As clients improve, so will their stories, he reports.

Maniacci (1988) discusses the role of writing in general, and stories in particular, in group psychotherapy. Stories can be used for both assessment and change. For assessment, themes and trends can be detected and elicited from clients' stories. As an adjunct in creating change, the stories can be psychodramatically presented with new and more constructive endings and additions incorporated into the "scripts."

Fox (1980) presents some helpful stories that can be shared with clients, and Berne (1972) discusses many fairy tales, myths, and life scripts that are equally useful. Psychological tests such as the Thematic Apperception Test (TAT) and the Draw-A-Person test rely heavily upon the client's ability to generate stories.

A young woman, in therapy because of recurring nightmares that were affecting her sleep to the point of disrupting her daily functioning, was extremely hesitant about discussing her past. She preferred to dwell on topics that were annoying to her, but safe and unrevealing. She admitted to having been an incest victim when she was a child but experienced considerable difficulty staying focused or dealing with the painful material that apparently surfaced at night in her dreams. Her nightmares, among other things, provided her with the opportunity to deal, in some way, with these painful issues without having to actually deal with them during the day. She was asked to tell a story about a young girl, aged fourteen or so, who wandered off to be alone with her thoughts. (Cards 16 and 8GF on the TAT offer a similar opportunity.) As the client related the story of this young girl, she began to project feelings and thoughts into the story that touched upon some of the painful material for the first time. The young girl had wandered off alone to cry; she didn't want anyone to see her. She was an only child who didn't have many friends. She felt hurt and alone. She remained a child who had been placed in a parent's role at home, and she was scared, angry, and feeling incapable of dealing with what was happening at home. The telling of this story brought forth emotion for the first time, an admission that there were painful issues that required examination and solution. The distance provided her by communication through storytelling offered her a safe and effective way of revealing herself.

The therapist may also tell stories—a tactic that will be discussed in Chapter 19.

RED, WHITE, AND BLUE POKER CHIPS

This is a specific tactic used in Alcoholics Anonymous (AA) for creating images. Bassin (1975) discusses the procedure in great detail.

When new members come to an AA meeting, they are told about the "passing the hat" ritual. Instead of making a contribution, they are told to take a red poker chip from the hat and keep it in the pocket in which they normally keep their money to buy alcohol.

After a few members have stayed "clean" for a month, they turn in their red chip and take a white one instead. After three months of abstinence (four in total), they exchange their white chip for a blue one. They retain the blue chip for eight more months, at which time they have achieved sobriety for a year. At the end of the year, they trade in their blue chip for a silver dollar with a one-eighth-inch hole in it. After each year of sobriety, another hole is drilled in that same silver dollar.

Bassin (1975) concludes that this procedure could be used for many problems other than alcohol abuse. Indeed it could be. Symptoms of various sorts could be recognized for being "controlled" or "imagined" for periods of time. In a more positive light, success could be the focus as well, with anniversaries for healthy, useful, productive actions being acknowledged.

IMAGINAL REHEARSAL

Preparation is required in order to move in a certain direction. The actual preparation varies from person to person and according to situation. For example, if individuals are preparing to *pass* a test, commonly they are studying and/or doing the reading before the actual test takes place. If others are preparing to *fail* a test, then a slightly different preparation sequence takes place. They are probably not studying, or if they are, they are preparing themselves not to retain, comprehend, or be able to express what they have learned at examination time. Preparation is usually required for both; the role of imagery is crucial in both.

Individuals use images and fantasies to facilitate or hinder movement toward goals. For example, as a conflict resolution tactic, such processes can be tapped into and examined in order to determine potential decisions. If someone cannot decide between his wife and his mistress, to use the previously given illustration, it can be helpful to tap into the imagery he has created and maintained in order to get a feel for "where he is at," so to speak. This is done in either of two ways (or both). Ask him what he imagines happening to him in the future (the time limits can vary accordingly). "How do you see yourself with your wife, say, six months from now?" If the images are primarily negative, some evidence has been accrued regarding where he might be setting himself to move. The evidence is reinforced if his imagery about his mistress six months from now is correspondingly more optimistic and countering. The negative images are facilitating avoidance-movement; the positive imagery associated with his mistress is facilitating approach-movement. Like any other tactic discussed in this section, the imagery may change daily according to the intentions of the client.

The second version of this tactic involves a lack of imagery. "Can you see yourself living with your mistress day in and day out, for the next few years?" If that cannot be visualized, there is a good chance that it is something he has not prepared himself for and is not intending to do. When giving the directions to clients, the therapist should be careful to phrase the imagery in such a way so as not to confuse one future outcome with another. For example, if that same client cannot see himself as being seventy years old (for whatever reason), then asking him if he can visualize/imagine himself at seventy with his mistress is not going to clarify the issue. His responses will indicate his expectations/intentions about living a long life, not his intentions toward his romantic status.

Imaginal rehearsal may also be observed in athletes who "psych themselves up" prior to their sports performance.

9

Encouragement Tactics

Adler and his followers (Dinkmeyer & Dreikurs, 1963; Losoncy, 1977; Neuer, 1936; Perman, 1975) consider encouragement a crucial aspect of living, especially so in therapy. Technically, encouragement is conceptualized as instilling positive expectations into the schematic framework of the person. With such a cognitive set, individuals are more inclined to engage in wider varieties of adaptive behavior with less stress and discomfort.

Maladaptive, pathological behavior is seen as a reflection of discouragement (Krausz, 1935; Mosak, 1995). A discouraged person will lack confidence, that is, experience feelings of inferiority and tend to cling to attitudes and convictions more dogmatically because the individual attained a false and elusive sense of security from them (Krausz, 1959). These convictions become increasingly rigid in response to demands from the environment that the individual is unable to meet and, consequently, feels less flexible and adaptive. The less the person is willing to experience, the less differentiated the attitudes and convictions, and thus, a vicious cycle is instituted. Encouragement is one of the key factors in both development and psychotherapy.

LESSONS FROM THE PAST

Clients coming in feel discouraged, complain about themselves, feel like failures, fear risk taking, and want to give up. The therapist may explain to the client as follows:

> When you were learning to walk, it was pretty risky. Your courage came slowly. First you raised yourself up against the leg of a chair, table, or person, and that not only made you feel good but it also got you the approbation of others. Having accomplished this, one day you decided to display greater courage and risk more. You moved from one chair to another, making sure that you didn't let go of the first chair before you had a firm grasp of the second. And that made you feel good. And one day you decided to "go for broke." You let go and away you went. It was a wonderful experience—until you fell down. You hurt; you probably cried. But I've never seen a child fall and proclaim "I'll never do that again!" After a suitable time children pick themselves up and try again and again until they master it. So, are you willing to display today the courage that you displayed when you were a one-year-old?

Other clients are often in a "rush" and need to slow down. They expect more of themselves than they would from others, and they typically treat themselves more harshly. Be it learning to walk, toilet training, riding a bicycle, driving a car, or some other task that took patience and perseverance, practically all clients have had at least some of these common experiences. As Krausz (personal communication) has cautioned, "He who is impatient remains a patient."

FAILING AND FAILURE

Many people assume that, because they have failed, it makes them failures. However, a distinction must be made between the deed and the doer (Dreikurs & Soltz, 1964). In a theological vein, St. Paul admonishes us, "Judge ye the sin, not the sinner." One can fail at a task (we all do every day) and still not be a failure. Babe Ruth was one of the greatest home run hitters of all time; he also holds the record for most major league strikeouts in a season. Using another baseball example, players with a .300 batting average command the highest salaries and the greatest fame, but that means they have failed to hit 7 times out of 10.

It can be pointed out to the client that there was once a person who failed in business twice, lost eight major elections in a 22-year period, lost his sweetheart, and in the middle of all this, suffered a "nervous breakdown." The client may be surprised to learn that the therapist is characterizing Abraham Lincoln. Dr. Paul Ehrlich, who won the Nobel Prize for discovering the first cure for syphilis, had a nonscientific name for his drug—606. Why? Because the first 605 drugs he tried didn't work. The book *M*A*S*H* was rejected by 14 different publishers.... The list goes on and on. Examples employed to demonstrate failing versus failure should be within the patient's experiences and interests.

Clients have a choice of how they view themselves. By focusing upon the negative they discourage themselves; by focusing on the positive and considering "failure" a part of life, they can encourage themselves. One has the choice to learn from "failure" or to suffer from it.

SAFE OR HAPPY?

Another helpful distinction to make with patients is that between being safe and being happy. Since life only rarely permits one to be *completely* safe and *completely* happy simultaneously, we usually have to give up some of one to have more of the other. Most people will agree that being safe is nice but being happy is better. However, the more one pursues happiness, the more it seems to elude the person (Sturm, 1926). Happiness is not an end; it is a by-product of what a person does. Frankl (1968) holds a similar view:

> ...pursuit of happiness is a contradiction. The more we strive for happiness, the less we attain it...the aims of both the hedonistic philosophy of the Epicureans and the quietistic philosophy of the Stoics, i.e., happiness...cannot possibly be the real aim of human behavior, and [it] cannot for the a priori reason that [it] elude[s] man exactly to the same degree that he strives for [it]. (p. 41)

Clients often labor under the assumption that safe is better, and some—especially obsessive-compulsives—hold that only *complete* safety, a guaranteed safety, is comfortable. Happiness usually involves some degree of risk taking. One cannot win the lottery unless one buys a ticket and a commitment is made. Eating the same food in the same restaurant week after week is perhaps safe (J. Edgar Hoover allegedly did this every day for his entire adult life), but the pleasure gained from tasting new dishes in new places can be exciting and fun. Watching a good, old movie time and time again can help us avoid the risk of buying a ticket for today's movie and not liking it, but "safe" can get very boring. Every now and then it is stimulating to see a new movie.

Risk taking is a part of life. It is considerably safer to spend the rest of one's life crawling than to attempt walking, never mind running—or diving—or ever, dare we say, flying? It is safe to sit at home alone (and agoraphobics earnestly believe this) but taking a chance, risking asking someone out on a date, can lead to a lot more fun. The risks we take are almost always outweighed by the happiness we receive, and the only way to prove this claim is to risk attempting it. So the question for the client is, "Would you rather be safe or happy?"

One therapist tells his patients,

> When you were four or five, you saw kids playing on the other side of the street. You wanted to play with them, but crossing the street was a major risk. You had to make a decision whether to be completely safe and stay on your side of the street or give up some of your safety and gain greater happiness. Back then you chose to risk in order to achieve greater happiness. What's your decision today going to be?

DEMONSTRATING FAITH IN THE PATIENT

Faith can be demonstrated in many ways, such as by being silent, thus allowing the client to find the words or answers on his or her own, as Job's "friends" initially did in the time of his tribulations. Instead of forming pessimistic prognoses, the therapist—by adopting the posture of "Everyone can be better than she or he is"—demonstrates faith. Rogerians accomplish this when they rely on the client's "growth forces" (Rogers, 1951). Rogers (1951) writes, "The organism has one basic tendency and striving—to actualize, maintain, and enhance the experiencing organism" (p. 487). One can playfully tease the client in a way that shows caring as one might do with a very competent friend. Choosing the right phrases can demonstrate faith as well.

1. "When you have…" is better than "If you do…"
2. "I wonder how you feel about…" implies that clients' opinions are valued.
3. "No, I won't. I believe you can handle it by yourself," if expressed at the right moment and in the right manner, can demonstrate faith as well.
4. "I need to know whether or not you are prepared to…" implies faith in the patient's ability to make a decision and adhere to it, and also that the patient's opinion is essential to the making of the decision. Mosak (1995) discusses the issue of faith in psychotherapy in greater detail for those interested in the more technical aspects of faith enhancement.

SHOWING APPROVAL

In 1957, Rogers outlined "the necessary and sufficient conditions" for therapeutic change. One was "unconditional positive regard," which he defines as "the therapist's willingness for the client to be whatever immediate feeling is going on—confusion, resentment, fear, anger, courage, love or pride…the therapist prizes the client in a total rather than a conditional way" (Rogers, 1986, p. 198).

Showing that the client has earned approval can also be encouraging. Of the many ways of showing approval, some are as obvious as ordinary and sincere congratulatory remarks ("That's great!") or pointing out accomplishments to others (in appropriate ethical ways). Having fun with clients, joking with them, can also encourage. By doing so we agree that "It ain't all that bad!" (Mosak, 1987a). Adler (1929/1964a) even congratulated people on the construction of their neuroses.

BEING ON THE CLIENT'S SIDE

This is not equivalent to taking sides with a client, although occasionally it can be. One of the earliest and most potent ways to demonstrate this is to use the word "we" (Künkel, 1939/1972). "We'll get through this... We can work on it... We're in this together."

One counselor applied the technique this way:

A sixth grader, who had been referred by his school principal because he was not paying attention in class, announced at the first interview that he was present under duress. He was not returning for a second interview. The counselor inquired what would happen if he didn't do his school work. Defiantly he replied, "I'll grow up dumb, but that's OK!" "If that's OK with you, it's OK with me. However, if you had paid attention in class, you would have learned from the Declaration of Independence that as a citizen of the United States, you are guaranteed 'life, liberty, and the pursuit of happiness.' And if it will really make you happy to be dumb the rest of your life, I'll tell your parents and the principal not to violate your rights of citizenship, your right to be happy." The boy thought the counselor "crazy" (O'Connell, 1975b), but was intrigued by his approach and returned for further therapy.

Listening, not arguing, with a client can be one of the best forms of showing that the therapist is on the client's side. Sometimes, just reflective listening (Rogers, 1951) and quiet respect as the clients tell their tales can help build relationship and encourage them.

SHOWING CARING AND CONCERN

In general, demonstrating caring and concern for a client means demonstrating politeness and a healthy interest in the client's well-being. Little things like passing tissues at the right time,* using active listening, making eye contact, remembering the client's birthday, and making sure that he or she is comfortable

*Resnick (1970), in his article, "Chicken Soup Is Poison," objects to passing the tissues.

can mean a lot. Inquiring about relatives or work can demonstrate this as well.

Offering concrete services demonstrates caring also. Offering to contact an employer, look for a homemaker, or speak to others* can be encouraging, as can simply answering questions about factual information the client may need to know (e.g., "No, that's not how you go about filling one of those things out. First, you have to…"). However, the astute clinician will want to avoid these with dependent and manipulative clients.

OFFERING HOPE

Faith, hope, and love—that is, caring—are regarded by Mosak (1995) as necessary conditions in psychotherapy. Adler (Hoffman, 1994) concurs when he writes,

> I cannot forget what one of my patients once answered when I asked him, "What do you believe was the reason that I could succeed to cure you after all these years of misery?" He answered, "I became sick because I had lost all hope. And you gave me hope." (p. 311)

Many clients often display little or no hope. They are often pessimists (Krausz, 1935). Therapists may have to counter this pessimism. If they engage in prognosis, they may be obliged to relinquish their own pessimism. Offering hope at any time, but especially in times of crisis, can provide encouragement (Mosak, 1995; Stotland, 1969). "Things can get better." "Believe me, you're in the middle stage of it. The end is in sight." Keeping track of progress, referring to past successes, and being realistically optimistic will offer the client hope.

A father was concerned about his teenage son, whose Hodgkin's disease was in remission, but the son felt that the father was overly optimistic and that he was going to die. The therapist suggested that the father buy his son a long-term savings bond for his birthday.

---

*Szasz (1965) frowns on the practice of meeting with collaterals of the patient.

MODIFYING IDEALS AND GOALS

Adler (1956) claimed that one reason for discouragement is that people set ideals and goals that are disproportionately high, making the likelihood of success slim. A client who attempts, after one success, to tackle major issues is probably setting himself or herself up for disappointment, if not failure. One of the most encouraging things a person can do is see progress and success. With each small "victory," confidence builds. This is especially important in working with mentally ill populations (Maniacci, 1991).

People who start out running ten miles a day will be naturally discouraged. They may repeat the same mistake again the next day in a misguided attempt not to "give up" and subsequently become even more discouraged. Soon they just entirely quit. Much of the same can be observed among dieters. Adler (1956) spoke of individuals' tendencies to use antithetical modes of apperception, that is, "black or white" type thinking. For Adler, therapy entailed learning to see "shades of gray." It is not "Either I'm thin or I'm fat" or "Either everybody loves me or hates me." It is a matter of degree. That is how successful movement toward realistic goals is achieved.

CLARIFYING THE MYSTERIOUS

In group therapy, this is often done when the therapist uses the strategy of *universalizing*. How many other people have experienced that? Labeling the "abnormal" as normal is basically the same thing. "That's not so weird. A lot of people have done that." Reframing is included here. "It's not that she's nagging you; she is just showing her concern," or "It seems like he does that to bug you, but in reality he's just trying to get your attention because he likes you."

Explaining the natural course of things clarifies the mysterious also. "After such a heavy bout of drinking, he's likely to have the shakes for a while." "I know he seems bizarre and a little scary now, but once the medication has had a chance to have effect, his hallucinations and accusations will quiet down." "A lot of couples experience this in the early stages of separation; it's normal." Such information will afford people a sense of healthy control and confidence because they feel usefully empowered and better prepared, and therefore they gain encouragement at difficult moments.

In earlier times, when mental illness occurred because the person was "possessed," it was important to know the name of the demon who possessed the person so that effective counter-measures could be placed in operation (Mosak & Phillips, 1980; Trachtenberg, 1961). Giving the client a name for his or her condition often takes the mystery out of it. If such a name exists, then some people have already been "possessed" by it, and doctors probably know how to treat it.

CHANGING A MINUS TO A PLUS

Adler (1956) felt that the ultimate striving of all persons was to move from a minus to a plus position. The particular form assumed by the striving varied—moving from feelings of inferiority to competence, from insecurity to security, from weakness to power. Turning a minus into a plus, often referred to as reframing, draws upon the tendency for striving and directs it toward a more useful outcome. An example is the client who complains about his wife's nagging. It can be turned to a plus by reframing it as demonstrating how much she cares about him. Anything can be turned around, even what many others might consider extreme. There is the story about the young man who came home with all "Fs" on his report card, to which his father replied, "Well, one consolation—with grades like this you couldn't have been cheating."

The client is encouraged when the once negative evaluation is changed to a positive one, and useless behavior is decreased as a result. A young girl who shows a test score of 30 out of 100 to her mother can be encouraged by emphasizing the questions answered correctly rather than those that were answered incorrectly. "You seem to have understood those 30 very well." The child knows already that she did not understand the others as well;

she needs little reminding from her parents. She needs encouragement.

Dick Cavett interviewed a guest on TV who remarked that if he committed a certain error, it would be disastrous. The world would never forget it, to which Cavett replied, "You're probably right. By the way, what *was* the name of the captain of the Titanic?" This tactic can be used in a number of variations. Whether it is the captain of the Titanic, the engineer who designed the Edsel, or the professional football player who recovered a fumble during a nationally televised game and ran the wrong way for a "touchdown," the effect is the same—the client's vanity, the client's sense of specialness, is sharply challenged, as are the client's perceptions of the significance of his or her actions to others. Krausz (1959) expressed the view that vanity was a central factor in neurosis and described "the commonest neurosis—snobbism."

The early philosopher of the Adlerian movement, Alexander Neuer, had a question that he liked to ask clients who confronted him with the "It's going to be terrible" type of statement. He would inquire, "What would a little bird, sitting on your tombstone ten years after your death, think of this particular situation you're in?" The most frequent reply—"Not very much!" This is a form of distancing technique similar to Beck's (1976) decentering strategy. While it may be distressing, it is generally not one of those very important questions of living with which people struggle. Such a question invites the person to assume a perspective beyond his or her own schema of apperception. As the client's frame of reference expands, the issues and problems take on a less catastrophic perspective. Hence, movement that is less wrought with fear and hesitation can resume.

For the therapist, turning the minus into a plus is as much an art as it is a tactic. One of the many possible examples is that in which a client describes how badly she or he performed on a first date. Saying, "Well, now you know what not to do on a first date" can reverse this. "Think of how much better you'll be for that knowledge next time."

One client decided to beat himself up, declaring, "I'm wrong about everything." The therapist responded with "Maybe you're wrong about that too."

BELIEF IN SELF

One common issue with many clients is the search for "proof." Before any important or perceived important action is undertaken, they require proof that they will succeed. They, in effect, reverse the scientific method. Traditionally, scientists start out with a hypothesis that they wish to test. They design an experiment and establish adequate criteria for evaluating the outcome. They perform the experiment, evaluate the results, and accept, modify, or reject the hypothesis.

Clients work just as methodically, but in a modified way. They begin with a *hypothesis* that they believe is a *fact*. More often than not, they start and stop there, but some go on to "prove" the fact that they already know. For example, a client feels that no one will love him. He acts "as if" it were true, behaves in ways that others will not find him lovable, and thus "proves" what he already believes. Evidence to the contrary is either ignored, brushed off as a fluke, devalued ("If they like me, there must be something wrong with them")* or spoiled (the client sets out to *really* prove to them that he or she is unlovable and succeeds by being a "real jerk"). The self-consistency of the personality (Lecky, 1945/1969) is maintained.

One tactic is to invite clients to stop looking for proof. If they look to the past for proof, we can remind them of the story of Lot's wife and the disaster she experienced when she looked over her shoulder at the past. Evidence about self-worth is not something that can be accumulated, like stamps or data. How the person perceives himself or herself is dependent upon what goals have been established. If a negative self-evaluation is the goal, then "evidence" will be accumulated accordingly. If a positive one is desired, then evidence for that is sought after and found. Since everyone succeeds and fails, what is chosen to be gathered as evidence is a matter of biased apperception (Adler, 1956). Clients can be encouraged to accept themselves first, and then they will discover the proof to support their belief.

---

*We sometimes refer to this as the "Groucho Marx complex." Invited to join a country club, he declined with "I don't care to belong to any club that will accept me as a member."

For those who have a religious orientation, an effective way of approaching this same issue is to discuss their belief in God. Belief in God is an article of faith, thus independent of evidence. There is no irrefutable evidence for either the existence or nonexistence of a deity. We take a position and then muster the evidence to support or justify the stance. If a person believes in God, no proof is necessary. If one doesn't believe, no proof will satisfy the skeptic. Wiesel (1972) quotes Rabbi Wolfe of Zhitomir, "I fail to understand the so-called enlightened people who demand answers, endless answers in matters of faith. For the believer, there is no question; for the non-believer, there is no answer" (pp. 87–88); or as James Thurber maintained, "It is better to know some of the questions than all of the answers."

Clients are encouraged through this means to believe in themselves without seeking evidence or proof. If they make the decision that they are worthwhile, they will find the proof to support it. Typically, they will even stop seeking proof at this point and just accept the fact they are OK (Berne, 1964, 1972).

> Spinoza understood the need for encouragement when he wrote, A man who desires to help others by counsel or deed will refrain from dwelling on men's faults, and will speak but sparingly of human weaknesses. But he will speak at large of man's virtue and power, and the means of perfecting the same, that thus men may endeavor joyously to live, so far as in them lies, after the commandment of reason.

Or, in the words of the Johnny Mercer song, "You've got to accentuate the positive, eliminate the negative."

10

Tactics Related to Anxiety

ANXIETY-INCREASING TACTICS

Occasionally, counselors and psychotherapists will want to raise the anxiety level of clients, especially when the clients become complacent or engage in intellectualization. They talk a "good game" but avoid making any movement. Physiologically, there is no difference between mild to moderate anxiety and excitement. The difference is a matter of interpreting the automatic cues. Someone who is discouraged is more likely to interpret those cues as something negative; a more courageous (the word "courage" is the root of the words "encouragement" and "discouragement") person will interpret it as exciting. A bit of excitement is fun; a little anxiety will not hurt on occasion—it may even help to get things moving.

The Saturday Serial Tactic

In the early days of movies, when children attended on a Saturday afternoon, they had the privilege of viewing a double feature, a comedy, a cartoon, coming attractions, the news, and the Saturday serial. As with today's TV miniseries, the serial was a full-length movie that was divided into 12 parts or "chapters," one of which was shown each Saturday afternoon for 12 weeks.

Each segment concluded with the hero or heroine in a perilous situation—the hero was hanging from a branch of a tree embedded in a cliff over a pond of alligators, with the branch tearing loose, or the heroine was tied to the railroad tracks and a train was bearing down on her. At the most tense moment the screen went dark, and the caption read "To Be Continued Next Week." In the ensuing week, everyone waited (anxiously) for Saturday to arrive. It seemed inconceivable that the star would emerge unscathed, although everyone knew he or she would; otherwise the serial would not run for 12 weeks. By the following Saturday, children could hardly wait for the theater doors to open.

The same process can be used as a tactic by the therapist with overly complacent, intellectualizing, nonanxious, non–working-at-therapy clients. A few minutes before the end of the hour, the therapist confronts the patient with an anxiety-provoking statement, interpretation, or question. When the patient, startled, reacts anxiously, the therapist looks at his or her watch and says, "I'd like to discuss that with you at greater length, but we've run out of time today. Let's talk about it next time. Until then, you might want to think about it," and terminates the interview. Frequently, the patient is on the phone later that day attempting to continue the discussion, but the therapist refrains. Generally, the patient arrives at the next session ready to work.

Some examples of anxiety-increasing closing statements might be "Is it possible that you're hiding something from me?" or "Do you realize what you just said (or did) implied? That's something we're going to have to really get into—next time."

Bringing in a Dream

Many clients report not dreaming, which is, of course, not the case. They simply do not remember their dreams. If they are given tactics for recalling dreams, they may bring them in. For Freud (1950), the dream was "the royal road to the unconscious." Other therapists regard dreams as useful barometers of clients' functioning and progress in therapy (Adler, 1956; Dreikurs, 1944/1967b; Gold, 1981; Mosak, 1992; Mosak & Maniacci, 1995; Rosenthal, 1959; Shulman, 1964/1973; Weiss, 1986). Clients who are not willing to share dreams are usually hesitant about revealing too much of themselves or do not want to pay attention to what may be on their minds, preferring to go through life almost as if they wanted no clues about themselves (for example, sociopaths). For those therapists who see the dream as performing a problem-solving function (French, 1952; Mosak, 1992; Shulman, 1973), patients who "don't dream" are usually unwilling to solve problems or to be aware of the problems they face, or they "don't want to cross that bridge until I get to it." Sociopaths, who mostly take treatment very lightly, generally do not bring in dreams. Postel (personal communication) would ask them to bring in a dream, and when they protested, "I never dream," he would tell them that he nevertheless wanted them to bring in a dream at the following session. He followed this with an "or else," such as "or else we will not meet." They almost always brought in a dream. Those who work with sociopaths will immediately discern that these may not have been actual dreams, but rather "made-up" stories. However, even made-up stories, a creative product, have some projective value.

The "bring in a…" can be used with virtually anything, from childhood photographs to drawings or creative writing. The goal is to raise the clients' anxiety sufficiently to motivate them to move ahead with therapy.

Setting Limits

Limits can be imposed in terms of number of sessions or with regard to conditions. For example, a prearranged time-limited psychotherapy contract can be a powerful motivator for a client (Ferenczi & Rank, 1925; Shlien, Mosak, & Dreikurs, 1962; Taft, 1933/1973). If only 20 sessions are set to accomplish certain goals, the use of phrases such as "Only three sessions left" can increase anxiety and invite the client to make the best use of the time remaining.

Conditions can refer to a number of available options, such as "Only if you accomplish the contracted for tasks by (this date) will we continue your therapy" or "The judge said you must be here, and I must report to the court. What am I going to have to tell them?"

ANXIETY-REDUCING TACTICS

Underexaggeration

Underexaggeration involves making less of something than it actually is. Since clients tend to be oversensitive, they are often on the lookout for certain things that create anxiety, and they are quite adept at training themselves to be overly sensitive to certain situations. In this way, they keep others off balance and safeguard their self-esteem. People in the client's social field feel that they have to walk on eggs for fear of "breaking" clients. Like the paradoxical technique, "When do we come to the bad part?" this tactic takes the wind out of the patient's sails. The issue can be acknowledged as "bad" but its importance is greatly played down. "So you forgot your speech. It's embarrassing, yes, but big deal. I thought you killed someone." "You didn't fail; you stumbled a bit. Nobody even noticed, I'll bet." "You didn't drop food all over the place; you were merely a bit sloppy." Ellis (1974, 1977a, 1977b) uses a similar technique when he helps patients understand the meaning of "awful," "should," and "must" from the sentences they use.

The essence is to change the "ego-dystonic" label to a more "ego-syntonic" one—or, in other words, to make it more acceptable to the clients. Whenever they think back on it afterward, it will be less anxiety-laden.

Naming the Demon

Similar to "clarifying the mysterious," this technique involves giving the client a label to clarify the situation. "That's not a heart attack; it's just anxiety." "It's OK. That's a normal side effect of the medication. Calm down. We'll see what can be done." "Look, here's what you've got to expect during the next 12 to 24 hours..."

Many times when sick, individuals are relieved just to have a physician diagnose the ailment. It is as if knowing the name actually gives the patient some sense of control over his or her destiny. The principal way in which this technique differs from "clarifying the mysterious" is in the inclusion of a label that clients can use to calm and reassure themselves in times of crisis. "OK, this is not going to kill me; it's just anxiety." Low's (1952) "spotting" technique and Gendlin's (1981) "focusing" are similar approaches.

A client came to counseling because she couldn't understand why she became so "upset" every spring. We examined her history, and realized that it was a rather significant time of year for her. Not only had she lost her parents in the spring (several years earlier), but she had had major surgery, from which she never fully recovered, a few years prior during the spring. She was experiencing what is commonly referred to as an "anniversary reaction," and once she became aware of it, she was better able to deal with the numerous issues in and around her idea of "spring."

Providing Crutches

At times it is therapeutic to support clients' efforts at denial. The material or situation may be too overwhelming, particularly in times of crisis. Much the same can be done with intellectualization and rationalization. There are times when it may be appropriate to encourage them.

Medication, a few hours of sleep, a "safe haven," or a promise can serve to reduce anxiety considerably, and at times may not be merely appropriate but required. Effective counseling cannot be done in cases of extreme emergencies (e.g., the client on the ledge of a building should not be asked to report a dream). Subsequent to the resolution of the crisis and when the client is again in control, steps can be directed toward change or the prevention of recurrence. Until then, quieting things down may be the most that can be accomplished.

Taking Over

Many times the patient will respond to the image of one assuming authority. "All right, this has gone far enough. Let's settle down now." Stopping the patient from getting more upset may entail shelving some issues as well. "Don't try to solve it now. We can get back to it another time." The therapist demonstrating competence can also calm the patient. If so, the patient will trust the therapist and the therapist's skill. "If you do what I ask, you'll be calm in 15 minutes. Now just…"

Interpretation

Anxiety, like other symptoms, serves its purpose. Adler (1956) felt that by revealing the purpose, the usefulness of anxiety would be eliminated. Manaster and Corsini (1982) describe anxiety as what happens when "*what is* is less than *what should be*" (p. 108). Another way of conceptualizing anxiety is to see it as an expression of inadequacy feelings. Whatever is occurring or perceived to be occurring is something that the person subjectively determines he or she is not capable of handling. Hence, when Adler (1956) commented that "in many people, anxiety means only that someone must be present to occupy himself with them" and that the person suffering from anxiety is therefore "blocking the way to further activity," he was speaking about the functional, purposeful nature of the symptom (p. 304). If a person believes, and therefore feels, that he or she is incapable of dealing with a situation, one choice of behavior is to elicit someone's aid with the task, that is, "someone to occupy himself with" or to withdraw from the situation, such as, "block further activity."

With these guidelines in mind, the therapist's interpretations can be directed to the purposeful nature of anxiety. "Could it be that you're so anxious because you don't think that you can handle this, that you can't cope, and you want some help?" or "Might it be that one reason you are so anxious is that you really don't want to be doing this?" "Are you perhaps trying to impress yourself with how scary life is?" Interpretations are phrased tentatively in these instances, allowing the client to react and modify them accordingly. Anxiety can be reframed as a weapon, a powerful tool to place others in the client's service, and, rather than seeing it as a sign of weakness, it can be interpreted as an interpersonal maneuver.

11

Talk Tactics

Talking is the psychotherapist's major tool; most of psychotherapy revolves around it. Though nonverbal communication is important and often more "telling" than verbal communication, talking is the basic tool by which therapy is conducted.

People are aware of the power of the spoken word in their everyday living. There are many different ways they alter their speech patterns depending upon the goal that they wish to achieve. Again, a teleological perspective allows much light to be shed upon how talking is used in various ways to communicate different things. What the person wants, she or he is striving for, will determine what language is used and how.

Speed, intonation, and power are three characteristics by which to examine the process (Mosak & Shulman, 1977). Speaking excessively fast can be a way of keeping others off balance. Someone cannot be found wrong if insufficient time is given to examine what is being said. It also prevents others from interjecting their comments. Listeners can feel overwhelmed by the pace and simply accept what is being said, almost out of exhaustion. Likewise, a slow, methodical pace can be unnerving or boring and viewed as a request to "leave me alone or else you'll have to pay for listening to me." The tone of voice also makes a difference, as any parent knows too well. And power is another key element. A whisper invites the therapist to lean forward and pay special attention to the speaker, and probably also to be gentle. A loud, boisterous voice may, literally and figuratively, be full of hot air, an attempt to impress through "packaging," not substance. "I'm not sure whether I agree with what he said, but he said it so forcefully." These are some of the issues psychotherapists ought to be aware of when examining their patients' speech—and their own.

ADLER AND THE DEPRESSED PATIENT

Dreikurs (Terner & Pew, 1978) related a story concerning Adler's interview with a psychotically depressed patient. Adler arrived at the sanitarium and started the interview.

> All the psychiatrists, the residents and nurses stood around in a circle.... It was an unforgettable scene.... He asked him a question about himself and the patient began to respond in the characteristically slow way of a depressed person. But Adler did not wait until the patient finished the sentence—and threw another question at him. Again, the patient began to answer slowly; again Adler did not wait and fired off another question. At this point, I felt distinct embarrassment. After all, Adler was my teacher...and here he was, apparently ignoring the basic rudiments of a psychiatric interview. Doesn't he know that a depressed person speaks slowly? Why doesn't he wait for his answers if he wants to talk to him?... Finally, I began to feel ashamed of him. When suddenly— to everyone's surprise—the patient began to speak rapidly in order to say what he wanted to express. (pp. 74–75)

What Adler demonstrated so memorably to Dreikurs and the others at the sanitarium was his ability to produce movement on the patient's part solely through the medium of speech. Rather than discuss the issue, Adler did something about it, and demonstrated, among other things, that "talking" could be used very effectively as a tactic. Though not necessarily effective or appropriate with a very depressed client, when used judiciously it can produce major effects.

ONE SENTENCE AT A TIME

For clients with "verbal diarrhea," that is, clients who speak too swiftly and produce too much information for the therapist to process, they can be urged to slow down. Ground rules can be established from the beginning—"one sentence at a time." Such rules can be explicitly stated and agreed upon, or the therapist can choose to respond to one sentence at a time provided the patient draws a breath and lets the therapist interject a response. If the latter does not occur, some therapists demand "My turn!" and set up the situation of one sentence at a time, explaining, "If at the end of your sentence I understand what you've said, I will give you a signal to that effect. If I don't understand, there's no reason to proceed to the next sentence, in which case we'll have to stay with your first sentence." This may be difficult for patients, but they learn to speak more slowly and to permit therapist response. When interviewing a manic client, the therapist's speaking slowly, softly, and responding to sentences or portions thereof can do much to calm the patient down. By refusing to "play the patient's game," by not getting caught up in the whirlwind of dialogue and flight of ideas, the therapist can slow down the client, much the same way Adler is reported to have sped up the depressed client's verbalizations.

OBSCENITY

Patients who use obscenities can be offensive to the therapist and to others. A helpful distinction for the therapist is to clarify the use of obscenity. Patients may be using it to upset, put off, or demonstrate something to the therapist. Its purpose may be consistent with the lifestyle goals of the individual using it. On some occasions, however, statements may not represent obscenities for certain patients but may merely reflect the culture or region in which they grew up. Obscenities may also be demonstrations of masculinity, such as, "I'm one of the boys!" (Mosak & Schneider, 1977). The latter usage is prevalent in the locker room and the military.* Obscenities by women are often a demonstration of "feminine equality" or what Adler termed "the masculine protest" (Mosak & Schneider, 1977).

The distinction can be an important one. It is equivalent to the distinction between being manipulated by the client and understanding and accepting where the client "is at." In the latter instance, understanding and sensitive prompting/reminding can help, especially since the client, at least initially, may not be aware of doing anything offensive; in the former case its purpose may require being dealt with in psychotherapy. The possibility of the patient's having Giles de la Tourette syndrome should not be overlooked.

SILENCE

Silence in the therapeutic interview usually leaves people uncomfortable. When the therapist is silent, the patient is often uncomfortable. When the roles are reversed, the therapist is often uncomfortable. It is especially difficult for young therapists to encounter silence, consequently their first temptation is to burst in and do something so that the silence will not be extensive. And yet, that may not be the intervention that is indicated. Sometimes one may be interrupting the patient's work; in his or her silence, the patient may be mulling something over, thinking about it, working on it without necessarily communicating this out loud. People often confuse being silent with doing nothing. Not so. Nor is silence always negative: That is often quite distant from the truth. Silence on the part of the therapist can be a potentially anxiety-reducing, encouragement, or paradoxical tactic, depending upon its use. Silence is not identical with being inattentive. In fact, being silent, as a tactic, is all the more effective if the attention is given to the client simultaneously.

In general, silence can interrupt the transactional game that may be occurring. The pattern, once broken, can be dealt with efficiently. For example, with the game, "yes, but...," silence on the

*See joke No. 88 in Mosak's *Ha Ha and Aha* (1987a).

therapist's part can dissolve the struggle and allow the client the opportunity to examine the present situation (Adler, 1956; Berne, 1964). Silence can also be a curious form of projective technique for some clients who will respond to the lack of overt communication in their particular styles and with their particular patterns.

When the client is silent, one must ascertain the purpose of the silence. If the patient is being reflective, the therapist may also decide to remain silent. If the patient is silent because of "hurting," an empathic stance may be adopted. If the patient is being refractory, multiple psychotherapy (Dreikurs, Shulman, & Mosak, 1984) may be utilized and the therapist can engage in dialogue to interpret the silence or break it. Sometimes the patient is silent because she or he is under the erroneous assumption that "one only speaks when spoken to." While the therapist is waiting for the patient to say something, the patient is likewise waiting for the therapist to initiate conversation. Occasionally the patient is silent because of a revelation. She or he has understood something that one minute previously had been a mystery. There is just one "catch." Having experienced this revelation, the patient doesn't know where to go with it. So she or he sits there silently, meditating, "OK, now I know this, and knowing this, what do I change? What do I do differently? What does it mean in my life?" So the client knows that it is important at some level but doesn't know important to what. It is not justified to assume that the patient's silence always reflects resistance and that one must overcome that resistance. One can often handle the silence very simply—"A penny for your thoughts!" In other instances, resistance may be involved. "With your silence, are you telling me that you're angry with me?" This form of silence is similar to that of the deaf person who turns her or his back on another person to demonstrate anger.

Where resistance is involved, many techniques for dealing with it are available. One can question aloud, "I wonder if the reason you're not talking to me is…." One can also add, "On the other hand, I'm wondering whether something else may be up." One can reflect a possible feeling. The therapist may wish to tease the patient but should only do so if it can be done deftly. "You know, when I was a kid going to school, they had a sign in my classroom—'Silence is golden. Let's all get rich!' I guess you're going to be a millionaire." Many therapists will feel uncomfortable with even minute periods of silence. Rogerian therapists, especially, will not.

SYMPTOM DISCUSSION LIMITS

One aspect of therapy is the imposition of limits (Bixler, 1949). Obsessive-compulsive or paranoid clients display willingness to spend entire sessions or clusters of sessions discussing symptoms or "problems" related to symptoms. Much the same is encountered in work with hypochondriacal and somatoform disorders. A simple but useful way for therapists to deal with such issues is to establish time limits. "OK, you will have five minutes at the beginning of each session to discuss your symptoms, after which we will move on to something else. Agreed?" One client was more than willing to discuss the events of the week for 30 to 40 minutes of each session rather than deal with some of the painful incidents from her past and from her marriage. Time limits were established; she was given five minutes to review the events of the week during each session and was assured that, after the allotted time, no further reference or acknowledgement by her therapist would be made to them unless they were relevant to the subject under scrutiny. She agreed and used her time limit well, thus allowing the session to become more focused in more rapid, smoother fashion.

SELECTING A TOPIC

For anxious clients, their selecting a topic can be a safe way to begin therapeutic work. For clients who have "nothing to say" or when therapy bogs down, the therapist's selecting a topic upon which to focus attention can move the session along. "Let's talk about anger today," or "How do you deal with your fears?" or "What was it like for you growing up?" are but a few examples of topics that the therapist can raise for discussion. Creativity on the therapist's part is required to keep the topics relevant and to draw the connection to the particular client's style of living. Once a good grasp has been gained of clients' lifestyles, consistency can be seen in many aspects of their lives. In group therapy, for example, raising the issue of dating and how individuals go about it will reveal different, yet consistent, patterns for each member.

Adler (1956) delineated three tasks of life with which every person must cope—work, the social task, and the sexual task. Dreikurs and Mosak (1966, 1967; Mosak & Dreikurs, 1967) added the task of self and the spiritual task. The person's response to each of these tasks will illuminate lifestyle issues. These can serve as good discussion topics. Some questions that might be asked are:

"What makes a man 'masculine' and a women 'feminine'?"

"How do you account for the fact that you've never been in love?"

"What is the most satisfying job you've ever had?"

"What about your work situation bothers you?"

"If I were to meet one of your close friends, what would that person say about you?"

"What sort of impression do you make on people when they meet you?"

The purpose of the topic choice is both to loosen up the hesitant or "stuck" client and to provide additional information that can be used for assessment and change. Selecting a topic teaches the client a skill that is especially useful in social communication. It may be of assistance to those clients whose complaint is "I can't make small talk."

REFLECTIVE LISTENING

Thought to be originally described by Rogers (1951), this form of listening is not the same as silence. To listen attentively and reflectively involves considerable effort and sensitivity on the part of the therapist. Dinkmeyer and McKay (1973) provide practical guidelines for application of this technique.

The therapist can use it with a client to help clarify, organize, and elicit feelings. When clients are confused and uncertain about their feelings, reflecting them back can result in rectification. It can build a solid, trusting relationship with the therapist and loosen up the client. The client may also see it is an expression of support, concern, and empathy. When a client says, "I can't believe she said that to me," in a despondent, sad tone, the therapist can reflect back, "You sound shocked and sad." That may be sufficient to commence working on an issue. At times it may be all that is required. Clients often experience painful emotions that therapists can do little about; clients' lives can be distressful. Reflecting feelings may be all one can do.

USING THE CLIENT'S LANGUAGE

Some clients like things spelled out for them; others need only hints. One type of client enjoys complicated explanations that go into great detail, use technical jargon, and "fit together" well. Wherever possible we use argot and idiom that the client recognizes. The therapist who attempts to match clients' verbal styles and preferences will generally have an easier time communicating with them. For example, a client with a Ph.D. in engineering is more likely to feel comfortable with details and having matters laid out systematically than a client who is an artist or painter and tends to think differently—perhaps more globally and emotionally—than the engineer. Interpretations and interventions should be geared accordingly.

What is being said can be greatly enhanced by how it is said. Using clients' communicative styles, especially their metaphors, images, and idioms, can improve the palatability of some interpretations and the effectiveness as well. An obsessive-compulsive client will feel more at ease with things spelled out. Histrionic clients may have to be "painted a picture." Through careful attention to the client and sensitive use of style by the therapist, clients can become more receptive in the therapeutic encounter.

"I-MESSAGES"

Gordon (1970), in his *Parent Effectiveness Training*, distinguishes between "You-messages" and "I-messages." "I-messages" can be used most effectively as a teaching device for clients. He, as well as Dinkmeyer and McKay (1973), provides descriptions and examples of their use. Clients frequently experience difficulty expressing themselves, particularly when they are upset; teaching "I-messages" can help improve their communication skills. Three sentence stems are used:

"When you...I feel...because...."

For example, clients who are having a hard time communicating anger can be taught to say, *"When you* fail to tell me what time you'll be home, *I feel* angry *because* I don't think you're showing me enough consideration." The first part of the stem ("When you") describes the behavior that is producing the emotion. The second part ("I feel") names the emotion. The last part ("because") tells why. Through role-playing and other action techniques clients can practice such skills and be assigned "homework" that requires their application in certain situations.

12

Reparative Tactics

With reparative tactics, the therapist determines what the client has been missing or has been deprived of and assists the client in making "repairs." What constitutes reparation varies from situation to situation, from client to client. The therapist either provides it for the client during the therapeutic process or aids the client in finding it on his or her own.

THE DEPRIVED CLIENT

The prototype for all reparative tactics is merely to help the client obtain what has been missing. To illustrate, a woman entered the therapist's office for the initial interview, sat down, and started sobbing. A child of the Depression, she reported through her sobs that she always felt cheated and denied in life. "It's not only right now either," she sobbed. "This has happened my whole life," at which point she spontaneously produced an early recollection. It was during the Depression and a group of her young girlfriends were standing around talking. "Let's all go home and ask our mothers for a couple of pennies to go to the store and buy candy," they decided. She went home, as did the other girls, and asked. Her mother responded that they did not have money, that it was frivolous, and that she could live without the candy. The memory ends with her standing on the corner as the other girls receded in the distance into the candy store. At this point in her recital she wailed, "Two goddamn cents! Two goddamn cents!" The therapist reached into his pocket, extracted two pennies, and placed them in the palm of her hand, closing her hand on them. "Thank God, you finally caught up with the rest of us. Now what do you want to do with the *rest* of your life?" She looked at him startled, wiped her tears, stood up, smiled, kissed him on the cheek, and proclaimed, "I don't think I'm going to need you after all." She never returned.

Clients can feel deprived of many things. Many, if not all, clients have been deprived of encouragement, which has already been discussed in a previous section. Stable, consistent authority figures may have been missing as, for example, with adult children of alcoholics (ACOAs) a genuine feeling of care and concern may not have existed (Kershaw-Bellemare & Mosak, 1993). The deprivation itself is not the crucial variable; it is the client's perception of deprivation that is significant. Many Depression-era children did not realize that they were poor since they had all the things their peers had, although that was precious little. Similarly, one-parent children will not necessarily feel deprived because they may never have known what it was like to live differently. Therapists should not automatically assume a state of deprivation if the client is not aware of one or it is not an issue in the client's life.

TOUCHING

Forer (1969) and Mintz (1969a, 1969b) have discussed the role of touching in psychotherapy, and Rosenthal (1975) explains how he holds patients. Ferenczi, who remained a Freudian until the end of his life, when invited by Freud to make modifications in psychoanalytic technique, introduced touching—a technique upon which other Freudians frowned. Arlow (1958) writes,

> Ferenczi did give his patients more than interpretations. He sat them on his lap, kissed and caressed them. This may be effective therapy—but it is not psychoanalysis.... Hypnotism, psycho-surgery, suggestion, inspiration, drugs, and electric shock are all ac-

cepted forms of treating mental illness, but they are not psycho-analysis. (p. 14)

Placed within the developmental context, Forgus and Shulman (1979) and Montagu (1955) describe the psychological importance of contact and touching for the infant. Harlow (1958) discussed the role of touching in love, based upon his experiments with monkeys raised by artificial mothers made of wire and terry cloth. Harlow had questioned Freud's theory that the origins of love in the infant were oral. Instead, he hypothesized that they were based upon touch. He interspersed bits of doggerel in his article, among them:

> Here is the skin they love to touch.
> It isn't soft and there isn't much,
> But its contact comfort will beguile
> Love from the infant crocodile.

The issue is that of touching—the effects it has when provided and what occurs when it is not. Many clients fear touch and touching and are poorly trained in it. Some have never even experienced a handshake. Like Harlow's monkeys, they reflect what may have been a deficit in their early training, and their posture toward the world may reflect it. As is evident in the case of Harlow's monkeys, the matter can be resolved through discovering under what conditions clients are willing and able to touch and be touched. This may involve risk taking and social-skills training. Sensitivity and respect on the part of the therapist is essential, as well as an appreciation of "transference" and "countertransference" issues, but as Forer (1969) and Mintz (1969a, 1969b) cogently point out, such care and judicious use is not true solely of touching but for all psychotherapeutic tactics. Knowing when to touch, and with whom, can be very encouraging and reparative for certain clients. Allowing them the opportunity to touch the therapist can be very beneficial as well.

Traditionally, the classically trained psychoanalyst considered touching to be forbidden and detrimental, although, as we have seen, Ferenczi dissented from this view. Much the same can be said of any technique under certain conditions and circumstances.

Shaking hands, a pat on the back, and a hug and the like—if used appropriately and with a client's approval—can do much to make reparations for previous deprivation. Touching and being able to touch reflect a sense of comfort and security in oneself and a trust in others that many clients lack coming into treatment.

Menninger (1958) considered touching as giving "evidence of the incompetence or criminal ruthlessness of the analyst" (p. 40). Rogers (1951) took an opposite stand when he described a dramatic encounter centering on touch.

> The group tried to be understanding of her and be with her in her feelings of being torn in two directions. I wasn't sure we were helpful. Toward the end of the evening, I found myself thinking about the painful tug-of-war within Michele. I felt a strong impulse to hug her. This set off a dialogue in my mind. "Isn't sexual attraction one reason you want to embrace her? What makes you think she would accept it when her greatest fear is of closeness? This is only the second meeting of the group and it would be seen by some, perhaps correctly, as a ridiculous "touchy-feely" thing. She hasn't indicated a desire for anything of that sort, so forget the whole stupid impulse.
>
> Despite these reservations, something made me speak out: "Michele, if I should tell you that I'd like to give you a good hug, what would you say?" To my amazement, she replied, "I'd love it." So we stood up and embraced each other tightly. I was feeling embarrassed, but somehow pleased that I had been able to follow an inner feeling, whether it turned out to be right or wrong.
>
> A few minutes later, I was surprised by her quiet statement, almost an aside: "Maybe I won't fly home tomorrow after all." I could scarcely believe that my intuitive impulse, so scorned by my intellect, had been so much on target. (p. 93)

In these litigious times, with concerns of invasion of privacy and sexual harassment, the prudent therapist may forgo touching to avoid legal and ethical complications, even when it is therapeutically indicated in the therapist's opinion.

RECONSTRUCTING

Reconstructing is a symbolic process that invites clients to recreate a situation to repair something that has happened. It is especially useful in concert with early recollections and the creating of images. For example, a client who is operating under the fiction that an incident that happened years ago is having an effect currently, can be "brought back" to that incident and given the opportunity "to do it again." Whereas in the deprived client tactic one provides what is actually missing—such as "two goddamn cents"—what is done with this tactic is at a different level.

A client, a young woman in her thirties, was still painfully upset by an incident that occurred when she was six. Her father had spanked her for coming home late with her little sister after school. She had attempted a new way home, got lost, and they both were late, upsetting the family. The "fact" of the incident was not the issue; it did not "cause" the problems she was having now, but it did symbolize for her what were crucial lifestyle convictions about herself, her view of men, and her view of the world. She was asked to visualize the memory of that late afternoon (she was both a very visual and an artistic person). First she "relived" the scene in her mind under the therapist's guidance, and she had no difficulty generating the painful affect. She then carefully recreated the scene again, with the therapist's guidance, this time changing some crucial elements as she visualized the incident. After much practice she was able to symbolically change the memory. It became one in which she still came home late, but instead of a spanking, both parents embraced her and expressed their concern and disapproval, but appropriately and tenderly. She reported feeling much better and relieved after the session.

The young woman's relationship with both her parents improved in the ensuing days. She reported feeling less tense and distant from them, particularly her father. Through the imagined recreation she was able to alter some of the fundamental attitudes toward herself and others. She gained more courage in her ability to approach people. Though much more work remained, this was a critical point in therapy.

Reconstructing can also be performed hypnotically. The thrust is not to dwell on past, painful experiences, nor is the client to be blamed for the current situation. The use of this tactic is to make repairs on specific issues that can then be used to motivate the client to make more beneficial and productive use of time and effort. The change sought is attitudinal. Once the client can change certain attitudes, convictions, or fictions about the situation, then therapeutic progress is on the way.

13

Trap-Avoiding Tactics

Since the personality is consistent, what clients do in the outside world will be reproduced in the consulting room. The manner in which the client deals with significant others will eventually be manifested with the psychotherapist. More often than not, clients come into therapy not wanting to change but rather to suffer less—that is, they want to continue doing what they are doing with fewer negative payoffs. They ask for drugs, for "miracle cures," like the ones portrayed on TV. They often seek everything but self-understanding, and with the current emphases upon biochemical etiology, these demands have become reinforced. In a way, clients are fighting for their lives; they are safeguarding their self-esteem and the way they have come to construe the world. Bugental and Bugental (1984) describe the fear of changing as "a fate worse than death." Challenging that can be most threatening to the client.

Traps are those behaviors or communications that clients use to defeat the therapist's purpose, and hence, the therapist, the therapy, and themselves (Kopp & Kivel, 1990; Mosak & Shulman, 1974). If the therapist "falls into one," extricating oneself can be very difficult, messy, and time-consuming. The best way to avoid being trapped is to spot the traps in advance, regardless of how well-concealed they may be. While this may not always be possible, the following are some warning signs and "set-ups" of several of the more commonly used traps.

"HOW DO I CHANGE?"

This seems to be a reasonable question until one examines it close-ly. Then one can observe it as a trap. Dreikurs (personal commu-nication) used the example of getting out of a chair to illustrate the trap inherent in this question. He would ask the client to in-struct him on how to get out of a chair. The client would tell him to plant his feet solidly on the floor and push against the floor. Dreikurs would do so and comment that he was still in the chair. The client would then add another operation—placing his hands on the arms of the chair and pushing against the arms at the same time he pushed with his feet against the floor. Dreikurs complied and announced, "I'm still sitting!" The client, usually frustrated by this time, would instruct him to lift his rear end as he per-formed the previous operations. Dreikurs would do so, remain in the chair, and only lift himself enough to lean forward, at which point the client, typically frustrated, would declare, "If you want to stand up, just stand up!" Dreikurs would then inform the pa-tient, "That is the answer to *your* question. Only people who don't want to do something ask how; others just do it."

Usually, those who ask "How?" do not want to change, at least not at that point in time. Like the situation with Dreikurs' client, the therapist can get into very confusing and detailed instruc-tions, all the while convinced that what is needed is more infor-mation for the client to change. The crucial difference is between education and motivation (Maniacci, 1991). With an educational deficit, providing the necessary information will lead to the de-sired change. With a motivational deficit, it will not. To respond to the latter with information makes the therapist do the client's work and may encourage client dependency.

"IF I DON'T LEARN IT, I MUST BE STUPID"

This is a deceptively simple trap. The client tries to form the issue into one of education rather than motivation. From a subjective point of view it is not that the client doesn't want to change; it is that the client feels she or he is a "dummy." In some instances the client has valid reasons for such belief in that the therapist is employing too much jargon* or not completely understanding the client and the client's language and metaphors. Barring that situation, such a response from a client is a setup for the therapist to feel sorry for the client, to slow down, to explain again, and to intellectualize while the client's position remains static.

An effective reply might be, "Now, it doesn't mean you are stupid, just that you've decided you don't want to change yet." "If you wanted to change, I have a funny feeling you would be able to understand it." "I wouldn't want to understand it either if I wanted to keep on doing it." The principle is not to get caught up in a discussion of the client's intelligence.

"I CAN'T HELP IT; IT'S MY NATURE"

With this response the client shifts all responsibility for the situation onto "nature." Similar responses are "You can't change human nature," "You can't teach an old dog new tricks," "A leopard can't change its spots," "You want me to turn myself inside out?" "It's biochemical," or "It's genetic." Variations of this gambit are to blame parents or to play Berne's (1964) game of "If It Weren't For You," all of which serve the purpose of thrusting the responsibility for etiology or change upon others. Sub-rosa the patient is actually accusing the therapist of being a "quack," for if people can't change, why do therapists treat them? This may constitute a topic for discussion, independent of whatever tactic the therapist may choose to implement. Discussions such as "the nature of human nature" or heredity versus environment admirably serve the purpose of delaying change. Avoiding this trap depends simply upon not playing the game, not "buying" what the client "sells," not intellectualizing, and not debating it either.

> "Even if it is part of your nature, you are the one who suffers. So what are you going to do about it"
> "Even if it is their fault, what are you going to do about rectifying your situation?"

---

*This need not be technical jargon. When Magic Johnson revealed that he had acquired AIDS through heterosexual activity, it was discovered that a large segment of the population did not know the meaning of the word "heterosexual."

"Perhaps a leopard can't change its spots, but they can be camouflaged."

"Even genetic background can be modified. You don't like the color of your hair? You can do something to change that."

"Even a person who doesn't turn inside out can still present the 'outside' (e.g., with clothes) better and perhaps feel better about oneself."

"IT'S A HABIT!"

In terms of metalanguage the habit in this pronouncement bears scant resemblance to the habits studied in learning theory. With "It's a habit!" the patient warns, "That's something I'm not going to change." If the therapist fails to recognize the meaning of this communication and pushes for change, the patient generally retreats to a second line of defense—"It's a *bad* habit!" and it is the conventional wisdom that bad habits are even more resistant to eradication than ordinary habits. If the therapist still does not comprehend the message and continues to urge change, the patient will retreat to a third line of defense—"It's a *really bad* habit," and the patient just knows there is no way such "habits" can change.

"I'M NOT PERFECTLY CURED YET"

This can be a trap in either of two circumstances. First, the client can be using it as an excuse for not changing, for continuing to engage in unproductive behavior. Second, the client can be relying upon it to continue (prolong) therapy. "I'm not 100 percent" (Mosak, 1967) is often a declaration that the patient intends to become what Freud (1937) called an "interminable patient." In either circumstance, the perfectly cured patient has yet to be discovered, as does the perfect person. "It's OK," can be the therapeutic reply. "I'll take a little less perfection and a little more effort every time." With a religiously oriented patient, one may point out that if the patient ever achieved perfection, he or she would be violating the biblical commandment that there be but one God. The therapist may also counter with, "Of course, you'll never be 100 percent perfect. If I thought it could be accomplished, I might strive for it myself." Or "Let's face it, nobody ever graduates from therapy with a halo and wings. Would you be willing to settle for a better ability to cope?"

"WHAT WOULD YOU DO IF YOU WERE ME?"

This, on the surface, does not appear to be a trap. It is. In effect, the client is asking for advice and/or permission (perhaps to reject it). The advice, more often than not, is the very weapon the client can turn on the therapist should the patient wish to sabotage the therapy or prolong it. "Well, I tried what you said, and look what happened!"

Teaching the client is valid. Many psychotherapies have a strong educational component to them. Educating the client is different from directing the client or calling the signals like a quarterback in football. The therapist may respond, "I don't know what I'd do if I were you because I'm not you." Other therapists respond, "I guess if I were you, I'd be doing the same things you are." The therapist may then cautiously add, "I know what I would do in such situations, but that only works for me; it may not be the same for you." That little caveat places responsibility back where it belongs—with the client.

"YOU'RE ALL WRONG!"

If a therapist is more concerned with being right than with the client's well-being, then the therapist is not being therapeutic. Being wrong is not the issue; the issue is the content of the discussion. "All right, I may be wrong. How would you explain it and what do you want to do about it?" The client should not be in a position to provoke the therapist into safeguarding the latter's self-esteem or reputation. This is a way of getting off-track and allowing the client to sidestep the issue. Should the client use the actual statement in the heading above, the therapist may observe, "Come on, no one ever gets *that* perfect!" The therapist must distinguish whether this statement is situational or appropriate. If it is the latter, then a discussion of the patient's sitting in judgment is in order.

In the clients' social networks, many people have been effectively diverted from potentially meaningful discussions and interactions through such a trap. They allow themselves to be hurt, they feel attacked and typically withdraw, and they leave the patient alone or fight back. None of these choices is appropriate for therapists. They may simply provide the clients with the excuse not to change. By accepting the possibility that the therapist may in fact be wrong, that the therapist has been wrong in the past and will certainly be wrong again in the future, the client is modeled more adaptive, useful behavior, and attitudes. The therapist who models *the courage to be imperfect* (Lazarsfeld, 1966) may encourage the client to give up perfectionistic strivings and adopt the same courage.

"YOU'RE UNFAIR!"

This accusation can disarm the therapist. If, with every intervention, the psychotherapist has to consider whether or not the client will consider it fair, progress in therapy will decelerate. Granted a therapist should be considerate and sensitive to the point at which a client is ready to hear something (timing). "You're unfair!" however, can be a manipulation of the therapist to turn over therapeutic control to the client. While the therapist should rarely control the client, the therapist should generally be in control of the process.

If the therapist has indeed been unfair, she or he ought to make amends. An apology is in order. If not, the therapist should avoid going on the defensive.

One therapist would respond to this accusation with a smile and the statement, "With all of the fair therapists in this town you could have consulted, you wound up with the one therapist in town who is not. Not only am I unfair, but apparently life is also. Perhaps we ought to take a look at your conviction that everything is unfair." Another responds, "I don't have to be fair, only therapeutic." Still another therapist observes, "Demanding that life be fair is like expecting a bull not to charge at you because you're a vegetarian."

FLATTERING THE THERAPIST

Adler (1956) spoke of the depreciation tendency, as did Credner (1936). In effect, the client will attempt to build up and then "knock down" the therapist. Feeling flattered is one of the surest ways of being set up. Adler (1956) relates, "A girl of twenty-seven who came to consult me after five years of suffering said: 'I have seen so many doctors that you are my last hope in life.' 'No,' I answered, 'not the last hope, perhaps the last but one. There may be others who can help you too'" (p. 339). If he acknowledged that he was her last hope, she would be in a better position to defeat him; he would have been accepting responsibility for her. His method for dealing with flattery was to place responsibility back on the client. The client was responsible, not he. He merely helped. "You're one helluva therapist, you know that?" is the client's statement, to which the therapist can reply, "Thank you, but *you* deserve the credit. You worked hard." If therapists accept credit and praise, it will facilitate the ability of the clients to stick them with guilt and failure as well. "You're so smart" can be turned around with "Thank you for saying that, but really, I'm like anybody else. I just happen to have more training in certain areas than others do. I'm sure there are things you know that I don't." If the therapist accepts the responsibility of being "so smart," then he or she may feel obliged to live up to that reputation and do more and "smarter" work than is necessary or therapeutic for the client—work that the client might be engaged in himself or herself.

Accepting flattery should be avoided because (a) the therapist can then be blamed for failure as well as "success," (b) the client may make demands on the therapist to do even better than before, (c) the therapist can be bounced like a rubber ball and manipulated by the client, and (d) the client can knock the therapist off his or her pedestal to prove that the therapist has "clay feet" (Mosak & Gushurst, 1971).

"I DON'T DO SECOND-CLASS THERAPY"

Resistant clients are viewed in several therapies from a social-interactional perspective. In these therapies, resistance may be conceptualized as a misalignment between the therapist's and the client's goals (Boldt, 1994). For therapy to proceed, therapists attempt to keep the goals aligned.

Even with such precautions, some clients pursue goals that are unrealistic and possibly detrimental to the therapeutic process or the clients themselves. In such instances, therapists can easily fall into the trap of being too acquiescent to clients' demands for fear of encountering too much resistance. A point arrives where the therapist may have to take a stand regardless of the patient's objections. A "No, I won't do that" or "That goes absolutely against my grain" can be countered with a statement such as "I feel, for your well-being and for therapy to be effective, this needs to be done (or stopped)." For example, assuming that the client insists upon individual therapy and the therapist honestly believes that group therapy is the therapy of choice, the therapist may explain, "I still feel that for you group therapy is the therapy of choice and that individual therapy would be second best for you. I don't do second-class therapy. If you insist on second-class therapy, I will have to refer you to someone who does that kind of therapy." As a Godfather tactic, the referral option is never accepted.

By reframing the issue as the therapist's attempt to do what is best for the client while at the same time maintaining professional integrity, the issue is not brought to a personal level. It is not a mere battle of wills. It is not necessarily the client that is the issue; it is the therapist's degree of comfort with what he or she is doing. The focus is on what the therapist feels comfortable doing and what he or she is willing or unwilling to do about it.

14

Change Tactics

If insight is defined as a meaningful experience leading to perceptual change leading to a change in the line of movement (Mosak & Shulman, 1974), then change becomes the necessary prerequisite to establish insight. Talking a "good game" is not the measure of progress; change in behavior is. Ways to help clients change are varied—in effect, an argument that the entire process of therapy is a change tactic possesses some theoretical merit. The process of change begins at the beginning of therapy; it is not the end point.

TASK SETTING/HOMEWORK

Mosak (1971) and Wachtel (1977) discuss the role that task setting plays in therapy. Wachtel argues that the integration of psychoanalytic and behavior therapy is accomplished through the assignment of tasks or exercises to which clients can then associate, respond, and describe their fantasies and fears. For instance, if a client has the conviction that "nothing ventured, nothing lost," a suitable "homework" assignment might be to risk something in the next week. Having clients read, approach other people, or attempt something different can be some of the tasks assigned. "Go out and have three meaningful contacts with someone this week," or "Tell someone something you've never said before," or "Next time she yells at you, give her a kiss" are illustrative of some risk-taking behaviors.

The tasks are very client- and situation-specific, depending upon the requirements of the therapy. Discussion of both the outcome and the client's expectations and fears can prove beneficial and encouraging. Tasks can be assigned for performance in the therapist's office or outside in the "real world." For those therapies characterized as educational or reeducational, learning is a crucial aspect of the process, and task setting can provide a vivid, in vivo, experience, much the same way role-playing can. Reasons for not completing the "homework" are fair game for therapeutic discussion as well.

An example of task setting involved having a client, a youngest-born who played the role of "baby" (Mosak, 1971) in his family, cook dinner for the family one night a week. This radically altered the family's perception of him, for the better, and his perception of himself, especially within the family.

Adler (1929/1964a) provided the template for task setting with the depressed patient:

> To return to the indirect method of treatment: I recommend it especially in melancholia. After establishing a sympathetic relation I give suggestions for a change of conduct in two stages. In the first stage my suggestion is "Only do what is agreeable to you." The patient usually answers, "Nothing is agreeable." "Then at least," I respond, "do not exert yourself to do what is disagreeable." The patient, who has usually been exhorted to do various uncongenial things to remedy this condition, finds a rather flattering novelty in my advice, and may improve in behavior. Later I insinuate the second rule of conduct, saying that "It is much more difficult and I don't know if you can follow it." After saying this I am silent, and look doubtfully at the patient. In this way I can excite his curiosity and ensure his attention, and then proceed, "If you could follow this second rule you would be cured in fourteen days. It is—to consider from time to time how you can give another person pleasure. It would very soon enable you to sleep and would chase all your thoughts. You would feel yourself to be useful and worthwhile." I receive various replies to my suggestion, but every patient thinks it is too difficult to act upon. If the answer is, "How can I give pleasure to others when I have none myself?" I relieve the prospect by saying, "Then you will need four weeks." The more

transparent response, "Who gives *me* pleasure?" I counter with what is probably the strongest move in the game, by saying, "Perhaps you had better train yourself a little thus: do not actually DO anything to please anyone else, but just think out how you COULD do it." (pp. 25–26)

Performing this task requires that the self-absorbed depressive "turn his or her eyeballs outward," a process Frankl (1968) calls "dereflection." It "is intended to counteract the compulsive inclination to self-observation" (p. 160). This technique helps such patients as the one who declined a cup of coffee with the lament, "I used to enjoy a cup of coffee in the morning but since I've been in therapy, I can't have a cup of coffee until I figure out what need I'm satisfying." Adler also invites people to relinquish the "shoulds" of which Ellis (1972, 1974) and Horney (1950) speak. Adler also suggests that depression is curable, a view that many depressives do not entertain.

The tasks selected should be kept relatively simple and should be set at a level at which patients may be able to sabotage the task, but are less likely to fail and then scold the therapist.

ACTING "AS IF"

Mosak (1995) and Mosak and Maniacci (1995) have presented a description of this tactic. The therapist presents it to the client by asking him or her to act "as if" he or she were someone else. For example, the client proclaims, "If only I were a real man!" The therapeutic dialogue might proceed as follows:

Therapist: For the next week I'd like you to act "as if" you were a real man.

Client: I wouldn't even know where to begin.

Therapist: Do you know anyone in real life or in the movies or literature who impresses you as being a real man?

Client: Yeah, John Wayne.

Therapist: Well, for the next week whenever you're in a situation in which you don't know how to act, I'd like you to act "as if" you were John Wayne.

Client: But that would be phony because I'm not a real man and I just can't be phony.

Therapist: I'm not asking you to be a phony. When Laurence Olivier went on stage and acted "as if" he were Hamlet, he was not being phony. He was acting "as if." That's what I'm asking you to do next week.

Client: OK, but what will that prove?

Therapist: It won't prove anything. It will give you an opportunity to experience what acting as if you were a real man is like.

When the patient agrees, the therapist may tell him the following story (see Chapter 20).

> In this small village in Hungary there lived a young man who was so ugly he was grotesque. He lived a solitary existence. The only friend he had was another young, compassionate man. One day the ugly man poured out his heart to his friend. "Why did God make me so ugly? I don't want to be handsome, but to be so ugly that people cross the street when they see you, can you imagine how that feels? Other people have friends and a social life; they get married and have children, pleasures I will never know." His friend replied, "That's a terrible plight but it doesn't have to be that way because there is a mask maker in the village across the river who makes masks that are so lifelike that you can't tell them from real skin." The ugly man protested (and here the therapist repeats the patient's arguments, "Wouldn't that be phony?" etc., and shoots the arguments down a second time). So they went across the river and the man was fitted for a mask, and it was true—you couldn't tell it from real skin. The ugly man returned to his village and everyone wondered who was this handsome stranger in town. He made friends, began to date, and life was wonderful. However, he knew this couldn't last forever because some day his secret would be revealed. Ultimately he fell in love with a woman and she with him. Life was glorious but it would all have to end because he could not marry without revealing what lay under the mask. Finally the day of reckoning occurred. She asked why they couldn't get married. He made many evasive excuses, but she was persistent. Pressed with his back to the wall, he informed her, "There's something about me you don't know, and if you knew it, you wouldn't even consider marrying me." She told him he was crazy. "I love you and I know you love me.

Why can't we get married?" "I guess I'll have to tell you," he said, ripping off his mask. "Now that you know, do you still want to marry me?" "Know what?" He turned and looked in the mirror, and lo, he looked just like his mask. And that could just happen to you!

Adler (1956) compared the individual's cognitive schemata to a road map, a guideline, which the individual follows as if it were true. Though the fictions the person follows are just that, fictions, the person clings to them because they serve to guide behavior and control and predict experience. This basic psychological fact is used to the therapist's (and ultimately, the client's) advantage. By substituting useful, adaptive fictions and constructs, the client is encouraged to engage in more useful, productive behavior. For example, we might tell the client, "So, the next time you ask her out to the movies, act 'as if' you were your friend Tom, you know, the one who is so great with the girls. Ask yourself how he would act in this situation, and then act that way."

A client at a psychiatric day center was encouraged to moderate her anger and aggression and to approach people in a more acceptable, receptive fashion. She claimed to be unable to imagine what other way to act and sincerely requested assistance. Her (male) therapist instructed her to think of someone who controlled her anger and dealt with "provocation" in a mature, sensitive manner. Her immediate response was her female therapist whom she still saw on a monthly basis. She was then instructed to act "as if" she were a female therapist whenever she felt provoked or threatened. She found this suggestion agreeable and easily assimilated the therapist's behavior, initially through role-playing and then in structured practice exercises with her social network.

As behaviors are incorporated into the client's lifestyle, confidence grows and the distinction between acting "as if" and actually "being" that way decreases. Slowly the clients become the way they imagine. Appropriate role models can be selected from anywhere, be it the client's friends or acquaintances or famous individuals. As the late theatrical director, Max Reinhardt, commented, "Always act the part—and you can become whatever you wish to become."

THE TEMPORAL SEQUENCE OF CHANGE

Clients often express the wish that they had been "cured" yester-day or complainingly ask, "Why does it have to take so long?" Often what is sought is a "quick fix" rather than learning something that will assist them to change. We explain to them the temporal sequence of change. Except for one-trial learning as, for example, in Saul of Tarsus' instantaneous conversion to St. Paul (*Acts* 9:3–19; 22:6–21; 26:12–18; *Galatians* 1:12–16), change is a four-stage process that is predicated on the notion of "catching one-self."

1. In the first stage, clients catch themselves too late, after having committed the to-be-changed behavior. It is similar to the feeling that French describe as *l'esprit d'escalier* ("staircase wit"). On the stairway going to bed after the party one thinks of all the witty, scintillating things one could have said at the party, only now it's too late. Here, as always, clients are confronted with a choice. They can declare themselves stupid, failures ("I'll never change, I'm hopeless") in which case they will discourage themselves. On the other hand they can applaud themselves for having taken the first step in changing, in which case they can encourage themselves. We inform them that people who are encouraged generally learn better and faster than discouraged learners.
2. We next tell them, "After you have caught yourself too late enough times (We word it this way to let the patients know that we expect them to catch themselves too late more than once and therefore not to disparage themselves when it occurs again), you will move forward to Stage 2 in which you will catch yourself in the act...and you will still continue to do it." (Again the phraseology is designed to prevent patients from denigrating themselves.) "You again will have the opportunity to kick yourself and tell yourself that you'll never learn or you can congratulate yourself for having moved forward to Stage 2. When you have caught yourself in the act a sufficient number of times, you will move forward to Stage 3."
3. In Stage 3, clients will catch themselves before the act but will generally, nevertheless, engage in the behavior. Again, patients

have the opportunity to encourage or discourage themselves, and again, we invite them to encourage themselves.
4. If they catch themselves enough times at Stage 3, they will be in a position to see it coming and this time not nibble at the bait. At that moment change will have occurred.

Whether or not research will validate such a sequence empirically is unknown, but it is not the issue. The issue is to encourage clients to be persistent in making efforts to change, to monitor their behavior and not to fall into old patterns "automatically" (e.g., "I can't help it. It's a habit"), and then continue movement. Some will leap from Stage 1 to Stage 4, while others will move from Stage 3 to Stage 2 to Stage 4. The pattern is not as important as the overall movement and the support and encouragement of the therapist and the patient's self-encouragement.

CHANGING THE RULES

Two stories illuminate this tactic.

> A tractor-trailer in a military convoy was speeding along a busy highway when it came to an underpass marked 13' 6". The truck was 13' 7". Nonetheless, the driver proceeded full speed ahead, getting stuck just halfway through the underpass, stopping traffic for miles around. The Army Corps of Engineers were baffled as to how to get it dislodged. The possibility of raising the entire underpass was even considered until a young boy, passing by with his family, ventured to call out, "Why not let some air out of the tires?"

Sometimes the answer is obvious to all those who do not accept the "given" limitations of the situation. Alexander the Great conquered the world because he did not accept the limitations of the Gordian knot.

Another situation involves the resident of Calgary, Alberta, who wrote the mayor to request that any stray cats in the area be licensed. The resident was politely informed that an English law, enacted by King Henry II prohibiting the licensing of cats, was still on the books. The resident provided a simple solution. Since the horses are licensed, merely pass a bylaw that in Calgary all cats are horses.

Both stories highlight one simple fact, namely that people sometimes accept limitations or fail to consider options available to them because of the manner in which the situation is perceived. Psychotherapists, in particular, are prone to such perception. Knowing clients too well, they assume that certain things are beyond the scope of the situation or the client and therefore fail to consider what would otherwise be perfectly reasonable or creative solutions. For example, clients can regularly complain that they are lonely, without social graces, and, in general, unlovable. An easy trap to fall into is to try to work with that premise. Like the Army Corps of Engineers, the therapist will be attempting to raise the underpass when an easier and much more effective solution is to simply tell the patient that yes, an awkward, unlovable person is going to be lonely. "So who says that you have to stay that way?" or "Why not become lovable?" can be the response. Rather than argue the point ("No, you're not lovable!"), change the rules, so to speak. If someone says, "It hurts when I do this," a common response would be "Don't do that!"

Counselors also may assume that the rules the clients establish are carved in stone. "No, I know him. He could never ask her to do that. There's got to be some other way around this." Well, perhaps he can ask. The counselor may be buying into the same rules the client has, and thus, be accepting limitations that the client accepts. It is one thing to understand the client's rules; it is another to follow them and not attempt to expand or modify them. As previously noted, the counselor must not play the client's game.

An example involved a client who was putting his family through all sorts of inconveniences because of his "ineptness." He could drive but he could not maintain the car because he could not put in gas or oil. He could wear clothes but he could not wash them because he did not know how to operate the washer and drier. He was too clumsy to cook or be responsible either for housework or yard chores. The family accepted his "ineptness" and operated accordingly. The therapist identified for the family the rule they had been following: "Johnny is a 'klutz.' He can't—

so we must." They changed the rule to "Johnny can't—or he won't." With some training, Johnny did.

Like the Army Corps of Engineers in the apocryphal story, therapists sometimes accept that the only way out of a situation is a difficult one. They are aided and abetted by patients who, when invited to change, announce, "That's so hard!" Schizophrenics, they believe, cannot be gotten close to or made responsible for managing their affairs. A dependent personality cannot be self-sufficient. An enmeshed family cannot have healthy boundaries. Because of such beliefs, elaborate treatment plans and procedures may be established and potentially simpler therapeutic avenues bypassed. It is sometimes so inviting to get caught up in the client's "games."

When therapy bogs down or when matters begin to get overly complicated, it is a good bet that the therapist is attempting to produce change by following rules that are not conducive to change. It *is* extremely difficult to "make" an isolated client social. As long as the "isolated" is accepted as a given, the task will be an uphill battle. If the client is willing to go out and make contacts, the matter becomes much easier. A "helpless" person will be very difficult to change into an independent person. The trick is not to buy into the "helpless" label and what that entails.

Therapists who engage in prognosis create another stumbling block in the change process. By engaging in self-fulfilling prophecy, they ensure that negative prognosis will come true.

At the end of the hour, a mother informed her family therapist that she no longer could engage in counseling. On the bus, her two rowdy sons ran up and down the aisle, knocking newspapers out of passengers' hands, and otherwise annoying people. When she attempted to control them, the other passengers stared at her with a look that accusingly conveyed "You're a bad mother." The therapist requested that she return one more time to discuss this problem. When she returned the following week, she smilingly informed the therapist that she had solved the problem without his help. Her sons had again misbehaved on the bus, but this time when people turned around to determine to whom these misbehaving children "belonged," she also turned around to look.

CONFRONTING CLIENTS WITH THEIR RESPONSIBILITIES

Dreikurs (1967a) would ask clients, "And then what did *you* do?" Quite often clients are very adept at pointing out what others are doing or have done, but frequently they overlook the role they play in the process. One witnesses this commonly in family counseling and parenting issues in which parents report what their children have done. "They don't listen to us." "They are so bad." "They fight all the time." "You should have heard the way she talked back to me." "He leaves every morning for school without his lunch." Adler (1956) noted that, if children are disorderly, one sees the shadow of another person who picked up after them. Behavior always takes place in a social field (Adler, 1956; Lewin, 1937). As a corollary, behavior and conflict are viewed interpersonally (Mosak & LeFevre, 1976). "And what did *you* do?" or "What did you do then?" invites clients to examine their own behavior. Along the same lines, asking "What are *you* going to do?" places responsibility on the patient's shoulders. Whatever "they" may be doing to the patient, what is the patient going to do about them? As Frankl (1963) points out, we cannot always control what life does to us, but we can always decide what posture we are going to take toward life events.

"What have you done about it in the past?" similarly confronts people with their responsibility for what has happened. It also implies a sense of potency and cooperation from the person (as do many of the questions in this section). Asking clients, "How do you explain what happened?" can be effective as well, especially if the question relates to their own behavior. "How do you explain the fact that every time she raises this issue, you get all steamed up?"

DO SOMETHING NICE FOR EACH OTHER

This tactic is a variation of Adler's technique to interrupt a depression. Coyne (1984) uses a similar tactic in couples and family therapy. Couples are instructed to do the following:

Sometime, during the next week, I want you to do three nice things for each other. There are two catches: First, you can't tell your spouse what you are going to do, and when you are doing it. Second, you can't tell your spouse after you have done it.

If the couple/family agrees to accept this task, several things occur. One is that the mindset of those involved changes. Instead of focusing upon the negative, what is wrong with the other or the relationship, everyone involved is looking for the positive, the good thing that is going to be done for them. Another benefit is that clients are usually pleasantly enticed by such an assignment; it can be fun to do and downright "sneaky" to do, like arranging a surprise party. Clients begin to think what can be done for the other person that is nice rather than about what they can do to spite, avenge, or justify perceived injustices. Rather than listing positive things to do for each other and then following through, the secretive element adds spice and spontaneity to it.

A simpler tactic is often prescribed in marriage counseling. The scenario involved goes something like this:

She (or he): The minute you come home from work you're grouchy, irritable, yelling, and taking out all the day's frustration on me. Well, let me tell you about my day! The teacher called to tell me that Johnny was in trouble again. The baby cried all day. The dog threw up all over the rug, and you think *you* had a bad day!

And the battle begins.

To counter this, couples are instructed when the partner arrives home, each on his or her side of the door should put a smile on. Then open the door. It is extremely difficult to fight with someone who is smiling at you benevolently.

15

Countering Tactics

Comprehending the basic premise from which clients operate can be very helpful. Ellis (1974) and his followers have presented and discussed in great detail ways of disputing clients' "irrational beliefs," that is, beliefs that interfere with clients' living as happily and comfortably as they could. Countering is one such method. Either therapists or patients may use it. Thoughts and beliefs that are interfering with useful, adaptive functioning are directly and actively argued against. Ellis even refers to such tactics as "counter-propagandizing."

Dreikurs (1953) speaks similarly of "basic mistakes," a concept that Adlerians have preserved but whose name they have largely discarded. One of the goals of their therapy is to counter these "basic mistakes," a process that others term "cognitive restructuring." Adler (1956) suggested that the goal of therapy was not to produce perfect individuals but rather to substitute smaller errors for larger ones.

There are many ways of countering such beliefs, some of which are discussed in greater detail in the following pages.*

---

*One counter, "spitting in the patient's soup," has already been discussed.

IDEAL COUNTERS

McMullin (1986) discusses countering tactics and notes that counters can range from one word to an "elegant philosophy."

One-word counters: "Stop." "Nonsense." "Ridiculous."
Phrases: "Forget it!" "That's useless!" "Not true!" "Why not?"
Sentences: "Just relax and take your time." "Nobody will care if you make a couple of mistakes."
Philosophy: "It's not who is right or wrong; it's simply a matter of getting the job done that counts." "At this point, what would be the best thing to do for all involved?" "Not everyone is going to love everything you do all the time, so you've got to do what you think is best for you at this time." "Conflict is just a matter of deciding not to decide."

Ideal counters are those that tap into a client's belief system and argue against it. If a client has the conviction that under all circumstances universal approval is necessary, one may counter such a thought with "Nobody gets universal approval, not even God."

McMullin (1986) offers five guidelines for the use of ideal counters.

1. The more powerful the counter, the better it is. "It's tough to be right all the time" is not as powerful a counter as "It's humanly impossible to be right all the time."
2. The more counters a client can produce, the better. For each irrational thought or belief, the greater the number of counters available, the greater the chances of the client's succeeding in disputing himself or herself.
3. Counters should be realistic and logical, not lies. McMullin notes that this is *not* always identical with thinking positively. "Life gets easier with each passing day"* will probably not convince a disaster-chaser to discard his beliefs. It simply is not realistic. A more effective counter might be "Life has its ups and downs, and some days will be rough, but others will be smooth."
4. Countering must be repeated. McMullin (1986) states that "It may take an hour a day for a year or more to overcome a life-long core belief" (p. 5).

*This counter is similar to Coué's (1922a, 1922b), "Every day and in every way I am getting better and better."

5. The counter should be in the same mode as the irrational thought, that is, if the client's belief is primarily visual, then the countering technique should also be visual. An emotionally laden belief would find its antidote in an emotionally laden counter rather than a cold, logical argument.

Ideal counters, as mentioned previously, do more than counter a particular belief; they counter an entire set of beliefs. A specific counter would change "I can't do this" to "I can do this, and I will." Label shifting is even more specific. It changes "ego dystonic" labels into "ego syntonic" ones. "I'm a worrier" converts to "I'm a concerned person." Ideal counters counter ideals—that is, systems.

Early recollections constitute one method for deriving core beliefs of clients. Ideas about self, others, the world, and right and wrong are given language and put into statements (Shulman & Mosak, 1988). Countering those statements, those ideals, is a major aim of some therapies. If someone is a controller (Mosak, 1973), then statements can be taught that will counter those beliefs. "I do not always have to be in control. Stop it. It only leads to more stress and anxiety." "If you were able to control everything, you'd be God and that would be a violation of the Ten Commandments." "Would you stop driving your car just because there are things on the road you can't always control?"

Ideal counters do not have to be the "elegant philosophy" mode previously discussed. Someone whose core beliefs center about being proper, looking controlled, and appearing intelligent (that is, he or she may never "kick around in the mud" with others by dancing, laughing uncontrollably, etc.) could be countered with such a simple statement as "Relax!" In fact, in this case, the more elaborate the counter, the greater the chances of its being used counter productively.

ALTERNATIVE EXPLANATIONS

One characteristic of the scientific method is generating and testing of hypotheses. Phenomena are observed and reasons for such occurrences are formed and then subjected to test. More often than not, clients generate hypotheses and do not test them. They act "as if" their hypotheses were the only true, viable reasons or explanations for the observed event. In reality, alternative explanations are typically available should clients be willing to decenter themselves from the events (Beck, 1976; Mosak & Shulman, 1974). Powers (personal communication) challenges certain clients with "Do you have a contingency plan just in case something goes right?" In many instances, the "truth" of the matter is not easily discernible, and the issue becomes more one of which is the more useful explanation to assume. Mosak offers patients who in TA terms feel "not OK" the following illustration:

> In your head and in mine there are ideas and memories of our good points, our deficiencies, our good behavior, our bad behavior, our successes, and our failures. If you focus on your good qualities, your good behavior, and your successes you will feel "I'm OK." On the other hand if you focus on your shortcomings, your bad behavior, and your failures, you'll feel "I'm not OK." You can marshal whatever evidence you want to prove whatever you want. So, if you want to feel "I'm OK," you can accomplish it by choosing to focus on the positives about you.

Sometimes this tactic is used in conjunction with the ten-finger tactic and the acting "as if" tactic.

In another example, a client discussed her fear of taking public transportation—buses and trains, specifically. She assumed that when she rode the buses, others were talking negatively about her. She would observe them whispering to each other and glancing her way. She was helped to see alternative reasons for why they may be talking. They could be commenting on how pretty she looked. They might have been wondering where she lived because they had seen her on the bus before. They may not even have been talking about her but about someone near her. They could have been feeling embarrassed and self-conscious and discussing *their* insecurities about being on a bus.

Another example involved a man who believed that he was turned down for a job because he was "inept and a loser." Some of the alternative explanations he came up with after considerable prompting were that it just was not the right type of job for him. The boss was a "jerk." The man was good for the job, but he had too much experience. He was very good for the job, but someone had more experience. The boss had two qualified candidates and flipped a coin. The boss gave it to a friend.

Again, issues of right and wrong are not central. Clients must be aware of the possibility of such alternative rationales. Once they are, the more self-centered, damaging beliefs, interpretations, and conclusions are divested of some of their power. As a countering tactic, clients are encouraged to generate as many alternative explanations as are possible for each troublesome situation. The stance is active and assertive, which not only dissolves the negative, useless-cycle, negative nonsense (O'Connell, 1975a) that clients tell themselves, but it is also preventative and self-reinforcing if done regularly and wisely. Before clients have discouraged themselves too much and become too anxious, depressed, or isolated, they can intervene on their own behalf at the moment the troublesome thought(s) arise.

Whereas "pointing out alternatives" is a specific confrontation tactic used by the therapist, "alternative explanations" is used by clients on themselves. As a confrontation tactic, it is used to broaden client perspectives. As a countering tactic, it challenges and modifies beliefs as well as broadening perspectives.

COPING STATEMENTS

Adler (1956), Ellis and Harper (1975), Bandura (1977), Beck (1976), and McMullin (1986), to name but a few, have discussed in various terms the effects of negative appraisal upon performance, specifically negative self-appraisal. Bandura explored the effect of positive self-efficacy on performance and detailed the detrimental effects of negative self-efficacy. What individuals feel about themselves and their ability to produce positive outcomes bears a direct relationship to their performance. Those who believe that they have little or no chance of successfully coping with a situation will often produce just that effect. They will not be able to alter the situation to their benefit. Those who do believe they can do something positive and that they can alter their situation typically will.

Coping statements can be a formidable form of countering, while ideal counters or alternative explanations may not always be self-directed. These two forms of countering can be directed to the environment and the situation as well as to the person. Coping statements are directed only toward the person. "I can handle this. I am in control and will get through this." Such statements are intended to decrease inferiority feelings, bolster self-efficacy, and dispute irrational beliefs.

Countering with coping statements occurs in three stages. First, clients "prime" themselves for the upcoming task. Second, they "talk themselves through" the situation. Finally they summarize and reinforce themselves. Professional athletes are some of the biggest proponents of this tactic. They often discuss how they mentally prepare themselves for the game/event by talking themselves through it, mentally visualizing their succeeding at the task, and then imaging and enjoying the results.

Practice is required. Clients may need to visually and psychodramatically rehearse doing such tasks in the session and then again at home or during periods of free time. They may have to counter themselves extensively before they are willing to believe it. As noted in our Guidelines in Chapter 1, "Believing is seeing!"

An example of using coping statements for countering involved a woman who was sure that she could not pass the tests in her new graduate program. Her mind-set was such that she repeatedly told herself (in not so subtle terms) that she was in her new program by "luck," that it must have been either an oversight or "charity" that she was admitted to the school. This attitude adversely affected her, particularly when it came to studying. Rather than concentrate upon the textbook, she frequently became obsessed with her impending failure. This elevated her anxiety, in turn making studying all the more difficult. Sure enough, she failed her first test and barely passed her second (that she passed was "pure luck," she claimed). Coping statements were combined with relaxation training and extensive rehearsing, both with her therapist and at home. Self-statements were modified from "I can't read this" to "Of course I can read this. Just relax." Instead of her telling herself she was going to fail every test, she told herself, "I'm nervous but I'm not incapacitated. I'll get a B with ease." After each test, she left telling herself that she had done "just fine, not great, but more than good enough." By the end of her first year she had gotten straight Bs. She started giving herself permission to get grades of A shortly thereafter, and she began to secure some. During tests she changed her self-statements from "I can't do this, my God; I've forgotten it already," to "Whatever they ask, I can at least answer well enough to get by." Within a relatively short time such comments shifted to "I know I can do this."

LABEL SHIFTING

Mosak and Shulman (1974) provide several tactics in this category. They speak of "clarifying the mysterious so that the patient feels less sick," "labeling the 'abnormal' as 'normal'" and giving the patient "ego syntonic labels for what he is trying to avoid." In ancient times, when belief in demons was in vogue, therapy depended upon identifying the demon, sometimes so that a countervailing angel could be called upon to effect cure (Mosak & Phillips, 1980). Many therapists still feel the need to name the demon. The various DSMs give testimony to that need. In general, this group of tactics is based upon turning a negative into a positive. Someone who dislikes many foods can be described as "picky" or as possessing "a sensitive palate." People who deride themselves with guilt feelings can be informed of their high moral sense, of appreciating the difference between right and wrong. McMullin (1986) lists twenty such characteristics and offers competing "labels" for them. The columnist Sidney J. Harris often published columns on "Antics with Semantics," for example, "I'm determined; you are rigid."

Similar to the pushbutton tactic, images that the clients create and the way those images are labeled can have a profound effect upon their emotional state. By changing the label of some key, crucial words, clients can change their attitudes and feelings. It is pleasanter to think of oneself as "helpful" than a "pest." The difference accomplished by such a stance will be noticeable when working with others.

As a countering tactic, clients are encouraged to catch themselves and are urged to modify specific words or phrases. A client who tells himself that he is "too much of a wimp" when he begins to become emotional at sad movies can be urged to think of himself as "I am just a sensitive, caring person." Someone who avoids fights and deflects argumentative confrontations could be asked to think of himself or herself not as a "coward" but as "self-assured" or a "peacemaker." As Jesus (*Matthew* 5:3–12) proclaimed in the Beatitudes, there is a great future for the peacemakers of the world.

SUBSTITUTING USEFUL BELIEFS

From a teleological, phenomenological perspective, individuals are striving toward subjectively determined goals. People who have common goals, such as to be happy, have various ways or methods for achieving those goals. For one person, to be happy might mean to eat a certain food, for example, chocolate. At another time, being happy might mean fitting into a certain style of bathing suit during the summer when going to the beach. If both of these ways of attaining happiness exist in the same person, certain compromises need to be made in one or both beliefs. Either the person has to eat less chocolate or wear a different kind of bathing suit or do some combination of both. A belief that might cause unhappiness is "I can eat all the chocolate I want and still fit into the smallest bikini on the beach."

From a more clinical standpoint, achieving excellence is a common goal. Problems arise when a belief that accompanies such a goal is that "I must achieve excellence in everything I do." Being the best is one thing; being the best in everything is another matter. A more useful belief that could accompany the same goal would be "I cannot give 100 percent to everything in my life. I'll burn myself out. Trying to be the best in everything wastes valuable time and effort on things with a lower priority in my life. I will take it easy in most things and concentrate my best efforts on those that count the most."

The essence of such a countering tactic is not to modify the goal per se but to substitute a more useful, pragmatic belief about how to achieve it. A clinical example will clarify the tactic.

A woman in group therapy had as one of her goals to be safe. She came from an abusive background where she learned quite early the dangers of being too trusting with others, especially men. Her belief about how best to be safe followed this kind of logic. "Being hurt by men is inevitable. I had better reject them before they reject me." Behaviorally, she would become involved in a complicated game of "Rapo" (Berne, 1964). "Rapo," in transactional analytic terms, basically involves someone first "baiting" and then "reeling in" another person. As soon as the person is "hooked" or on the verge of it, the game player rejects the other and "cuts the line," so to speak. This client would play such a game, and "reject them before they reject me" was her motto. Ironically, such a game got serious when she teased and hurt someone who hurt her in return, only worse. She managed to reproduce exactly what she was trying so desperately to avoid. Trying not to get hurt hurt her. A more useful belief for achieving the same goal of safety was "I will get involved with others. That's a normal part of life. I will be safe if I get involved *slowly* and maintain a certain distance emotionally, going carefully into relationships and taking my time." This phrase was repeated and repeated and practiced numerous times. Such situations was rehearsed in detail.

In these instances the goals the clients choose are usually appropriate. The problems arise in the implementation of the methods to achieve them. Asking the clients if particular beliefs will help or hinder them in their striving and then examining and substituting more practical methods is the issue. "If your goal is to be popular, what are some of the more useful ways of accomplishing that?"

However, sometimes the goals themselves are not attainable, yet the client hangs on to the underlying belief. Consider, once again, the compulsive cleaner who at five in the morning is on a ladder washing the ceiling because she wants her house to be "clean" in the event someone visits the next day. We can present the following counter to her. "As hard as you may try to get all your work done and your house clean, the day after you die, there's going to be some left over. Those who come to pay their condolences will probably find some dust floating around. Consequently, the question is not whether there will be anything left over, but what will be left over. That way you can choose what you would like to leave over until tomorrow and get some rest today."

PAST SUCCESSES

This tactic is related to the encouragement tactic of "using lessons from the past." When this is utilized to encourage, it points out the successes the client has had and how difficult achieving those successes may have been. It offers a change in perspective. As a countering tactic, it has a more specific use.

Clients often complain that they are incapable of doing something. This perception may or may not be true, but they believe it is. In ways characteristic of the self-fulfilling prophecy (Merton, 1948), they create experiences that validate their expectations. Ask clients to think back and recall an incident in which they did succeed at a particular task similar to the one that they feel incapable of doing. Next, have them think of a similar experience in which they did not succeed in the task. Compare the two and discover what the difference is between them. Typically, there are a set of assumptions or self-statements that can be isolated in both cases. The client can then be instructed to substitute the more efficacious dialogue of the success experience for the negative, self-defeating dialogue of the "failure."

For example, a client discussed his inability to deal with "authority figures," such as his father and his boss. He related an instance in which his boss, whom he rarely had to work with directly, called him into the office and asked him personally to carry out some assignment. The client became so tense and anxious that he failed to attend accurately to some directions, and he wound up "blowing" the assignment. The therapist asked him to think back and remember a time he had dealt with an authority figure and had not been anxious. The client related a story about how he had happened to run into his boss in the hall during a "break," and the two got along fairly well.

Both situations were examined in detail. In the first, anxiety-filled encounter, the client managed to identify these self-statements. "Oh no! He wants me to do something. I know what always happens. I"ll blow it and make and ass of myself." The underlying belief was one of his core convictions: "I'm OK as long as no one expects too much of me. Leave me on my own, and I'll be fine." This client's success had been as a security guard during a late shift in a large office building. It was the most successful job he had ever had. The second scenario he recounted, about the meeting with his boss during a "break," contained these self-statements: "We're equals. He thinks I'm all right and doesn't expect me to do something." The second set of statements was substituted for the first, with slight modification: "We're equals. He wants me to do something but he likes me whether I do it or not." This worked. He was relaxed enough with this statement to interact with his boss *and* pay enough attention to what was being asked. With repeated exposure and practice, the client was able to counter his negative beliefs with more positive ones that he derived from his own experiences.

This method can be embellished when used in combination with "creating images." During World War II, a fellow GI provided HM with a method of avoiding anxiety-laden situations with commanding officers. "Just close your eyes for a moment when standing at attention in front of the captain and imagine him standing around in his long johns with the trap door open. Remember, however, to restrain yourself from laughing openly."

Unlike acting "as if," clients with this particular tactic are asked to employ their own experiences and, whenever possible, the self-statements derived from their previous experiences. Acting "as if" typically entails modeling someone else's behavior, while coping statements usually involves generic, impersonal statements that the client adopts from the coaching of the clinician. "Past successes" draws upon what the client has experienced firsthand as a success. Should the client be unable—or more likely, unwilling—to produce a positive experience to counter the negative one, then the therapist can resort to either of the two other methods.

16

Logical Analysis Tactics

Psychotherapists have long asserted that in order to produce client change, one must first understand the client, then help the client to understand himself or herself, and finally work to change certain attitudes, beliefs, and behaviors. Adler (1956), Beck (1976), Berne (1972), Dreikurs (1967a, 1973), Ellis and Harper (1975), Frankl (1985), Mahoney (1980), Rokeach (1964), and hosts of others have detailed and examined various ways of modifying the beliefs of people. What all these theorists and therapists share in common is the belief that, by examining the cognitions, the thoughts and ideas of clients, useful, meaningful behavior change can occur.

Logical analysis can be a demanding and time-consuming form of working on clients' belief systems, but if done properly, can be very productive. For Adler (1956), the client had assumed too personal a perspective toward the challenges of life. As Dreikurs expanded on Adler's work, he noted that individuals who become discouraged in finding a place with others seek goals that compensate for this feeling of not belonging. Beck (1976) and Ellis and Harper (1975) both have detailed how automatic, irrational thoughts often interfere with commonsense, logical thinking. Frankl (1963) speaks of meanings clients give to events and life, meanings that sometimes cause more trouble than they are worth. Berne (1964) describes games and scripts that have losing outcomes built into them, but people do not take time to examine and think through the implications of their attitudes and choices. Gushurst (1978), Mahoney (1980), and Mosak (1978) speak of assumptive worlds that are simply accepted as being true by some people, even in the face of evidence to the contrary.

All of these theorists have tapped into similar principles and dynamics. The scripts, lifestyles, and beliefs of individuals are not in line with what the general, consensual view would be, and therefore, trouble is likely to occur. The tactics of logical analysis all have one thing in common—the clinician steps into the client's private, personal belief system and works to bring the illogical, irrational, mistaken conviction under close scrutiny, and to have the clients examine those beliefs in the light of commonsense, consensual interpretations.

FOCUSING UPON THE BELIEF

Clients frequently state things in shadowy, imprecise terms. By failing to clearly state and become cognizant of what is happening with them, they encounter difficulty thinking logically about it. "I'm scared" is a common expression heard from children. Almost inevitably, a parent will follow such a statement with two very important words—"Of what?" That question can work wonders in clarifying and eventually rectifying the situation. Once the parent knows what the child is afraid of, then appropriate action can be undertaken.

Much the same can occur in psychotherapy, but because the client is typically at a different stage cognitively and emotionally (at least linguistically), the process can be even more precise and rigorous. "I'm angry," while expressive, is difficult to work with in more than an empathetic, reflective way. "What are you angry about?" Or "With whom are you angry?" opens the door for further investigation. "I'm angry" can then become "I'm angry with my husband" or "I'm angry about not getting that raise." Another clarification for the client may be, whenever a person says, "I'm angry," she or he is really saying. "There's something about this person or situation I would like to change." The serenity prayer of St. Francis of Assisi (the AA Prayer) may be invoked here.

On another level, once the feeling or attitude has been clarified, therapist and client can focus on the belief. Identifying that "I'm aggravated because I didn't do as well as I should" can lead to an underlying belief that is being unconsciously asserted: "I should be perfect or at least better than other people." If this statement is the underlying assertion, this may be a good place to start work.

Horney (1950) was one of the first to describe such beliefs that can lead to anxiety and disrupt functioning. She referred to them as the "tyranny of the shoulds." Ellis and Harper (1975) and the School of Rational-Emotive Therapy have constructed an entire system of analysis of just such claims. Some "neurotic claims," as Horney refers to them, include the following:

1. Statement: "No one ever listens to me."
    Possibly underlying belief: "I should be heeded. It's a disaster if I'm not listened to."
2. Statement: "I hate mistakes."
    Possibly underlying belief: Things (or I) should be perfect."
3. Statement: "I can't dance."
    Possibly underlying belief: "I have two left feet." "I will only do what is proper." "I am ashamed of my body."
4. Statement: "I'm afraid of it."
    Possibly underlying belief: "I don't want to do it. Therefore, I will scare myself away." "What I can't control I had better avoid."

Once clients learn to state clearly what is being experienced, they can often be taught to analyze their beliefs on their own. It is a short step from "I'm worried because I don't think I can do it" to "I guess that's calling myself inferior again."

The process most frequently encountered is the identification of the emotion either through introspection or by observing physiological cues, the expression of the emotion, its clarification, and then the focus upon the belief (Gendlin, 1981). "I can tell because I'm clenching my teeth and my stomach is killing me. What am I mad at? He wants me to do more work. It wasn't good enough the first time. Here I go again, thinking I can do everything right the first time I try it. That belief has caused me trouble before."

DEFINING TERMS

McMullin (1986) presents a form of this tactic, but its roots go back to theorists such as Adler (1956) and Horney (1950). Beck (1976) has written about looking for overgeneralizations and distortions of logic, and Mosak (1995) has written on similar themes found in lifestyle assessments.

An apparently simple statement such as "Men shouldn't be emotional," when broken down into its precise meaning and analyzed, can be demonstrated to be quite illogical and even downright nonsensical. Mosak (1987b) has used the counter of "Jesus wept" (*John* 11:35) with religious male patients. For example, clients can be asked to define each word precisely. What makes someone a man? Age, maturity (try to define *that* term), puberty, a job, a wife, anatomy? What about the word "shouldn't"? Does that signify that they do but ought not to? Does it mean that they actually don't? Does it mean that they do but they should keep it from public display? And what about "be?" Can a man "act" emotional and not *be* emotional? What's "emotional?" Crying, laughing, weeping, loving? Should men act or feel like robots or computers?

Once each word is defined, the definitions may be summarized, perhaps as follows: "A man, someone over the age of 18 who has a penis, ought not to exhibit or feel more than three laughs, one sigh, or sadness of any kind for more than 40 minutes; otherwise it is wrong according to standards of the majority of males in this country born between 1888 and 1960." Ludicrous? Of course! That is the purpose of the tactic. Clients can be shown the extent to which they can tie themselves in knots over apparently arbitrary distinctions. If they ever stopped to take a long, hard look at some of their beliefs, they would be amazed at their conclusions.

When the process has been clearly defined, it is easy to find expectations and contradictions—even in the expanded, detailed versions of the "rules." "So, if your mother dies tomorrow, quite unexpectedly, you wouldn't shed a tear? You wouldn't feel upset for more than 20 minutes, if that?" "What about someone who is not quite 18, let's say he's 17 years, 10 months? Can he cry?" "What if your wife told you she would leave you unless you showed her more emotion daily?" "What if someone offered you a million dollars a year for the rest of your life if you cried once a month? Would you do it then?" And so forth.

This is more than an academic exercise, and clients can be reminded of that each step along the way. It is their thoughts that are being examined. It can be very facilitating in getting clients to analyze and question some basic assumption about themselves in critical rather than superficial fashion. They are thus given the opportunity to change these assumptions and not simply follow them blindly, day in, or day out.

DISTANCING TACTIC

Beck (1976) and Berne (1972) present the clearest examples of this tactic. In some ways this tactic bears striking resemblance to both some of the placing in perspective tactics and humor tactics. Berne (1972), in *What Do You Say After You Say Hello?* uses the term, "Martian." He asks his readers to pretend that they are from another planet and that little, if anything, is understood about life on Earth. What would a Martian, looking at this situation/encounter, think? Remember, the Martian knows little about the way human beings interact or think, so everything must be spelled out, even what is obvious to human beings.

What distinguishes this from a perspective-taking tactic is that beyond *assuming* another perspective, what is normally taken for granted must be explained and attended to. What is normally overlooked or not given much thought must be justified and examined. An example will clarify the process.

A woman in her early forties inquired about her experiences in managing her teenage son. She and her husband had been having trouble with the boy for months. She was very adept at detailing the scene from her perspective, with all the admittedly dramatic sighs and claims of exasperation thrown in to boot. She was asked to retell her tale from the perspective of a Martian. Though initially hesitant, she soon, with some practice, warned up to the task. Her story went something like this:

First, it is Saturday morning. These three Earth creatures get up, perform some strange ritual in these strange rooms that have water in them, and then gather around the table in the downstairs room with odd machines in it. It appears that the older male and the younger male are in some kind of competition for the attention of the female. She moves back and forth between them and eventually sides with the weaker of the two, generally the smaller. At such a time, the larger male withdraws and isolates himself, appearing disturbed and obviously more in need of attention. She then moves with him....

This distancing tactic permitted her to watch some of the transactions that occurred in the family. Despite the seriousness of the situation, she found herself inexplicably laughing at the process. Her Martian perspective led her to another interesting insight. "The smaller one is engaged in a form of paying rent, which is quite different from either of the other two. The large male leaves every day. Presumably whatever he does or wherever he goes, this is his share of the load. The female arranges things and provides the food. The smaller male allows himself to be abused by the other male (and female, occasionally). In return, he does less work but receives equal, if not greater, benefits than the rest." She was able to use this style of distancing to deal with a number of different problems. For this particular client, it proved very advantageous in helping her to see and examine some unspoken processes.

On a cognitive level, this tactic, like "defining terms," asks clients to think about and explain what is normally taken for granted. Although requiring some coaching from the therapist, it can be very revealing.

Beck (1976) asks clients to make a distinction between what they know and what they believe. That very process itself yields good results, allowing clients to "step back" and question the validity and evidence for their assumptions. As an example, he presents the woman who suffered from chronic anxiety. She would see things and immediately assume the worst. If, driving down the street where she resided, she saw smoke and fire trucks, she would say to herself, "My house is on fire." she was encouraged to think, "I think it might be my house. It doesn't have to be." Her anxiety began to diminish.

SEEING CONNECTIONS

Many clients multiply the number of problems they have. If they were to work on them one by one, the therapeutic task would become endless. In a film, *The Case of Bill* (Mosak, 1979), the client indicates on initial interview that he has "a million problems." This already is an invitation for an extended therapy. The therapist replies "No, you have only one problem with a million variations." The therapy is now a bit more manageable.

Clients fail to see the connection between events and outcomes. Most significantly, clients typically fail to see the connection between their processes (beliefs, attitudes, behaviors, and emotions) and those processes in their social field. McMullin (1986) presents a generic, abstract example of a tactic he calls "forming hypotheses."

> What is Alfred afraid of?
> The Facts: He is afraid of the cocker spaniel.
> He is not afraid of the fish.
> Alfred is afraid of rabbits.
> He is afraid of dogs.
> He is not afraid of parakeets.
> Alfred is not afraid of roaches.
> He is afraid of his mother's mink coat.
> He is not afraid of his dad's leather vest.
> He is afraid of bears. (p. 243)

The client is then asked to deduce from the evidence what Alfred is afraid of. The answer: Fur. Some clients assume that they are afraid of dogs, rabbits, mink coats, and bears, thus feeling helpless and even more overwhelmed by their fears, when in reality they are merely afraid of fur. It is not necessarily that they have learned to think inductively but rather that they have begun to think in terms of a gestalt, that is, to look for patterns and recurrent themes. This allows them to begin to get a handle on their lives and see the coherence. It is also easier when dealing with one class of attitudes that have many facets (like fur and fur-related items) rather than with each individual facet consecutively.

In a more clinically applicable and recognizable form, a client may be concerned with the following problems:

I can't get along with people at work.
My wife and I are distant.
I get along well with my children.
I hate (passionately) puzzles or brainteasers.
Sexually, I enjoy intercourse or foreplay only when I initiate it.

The connection could be that he enjoys himself only when he feels he is in control. He cannot control his wife and coworkers. His children, he can. When he initiates sex, he calls the shots.

Through logical analysis, connections can be made that will make the formerly long list of complaints more manageable. The client will be able to cluster his or her symptoms and reduce the magnitude of his or her symptomology.

TRACKING BELIEFS

Tracking beliefs has a specific, analyzable connotation. Once clients have become adept at identifying particular beliefs, they are trained to examine their thoughts and define their terms. With distancing, clients can observe their overinvolvement in their problems and, in doing so, lose perspective. If they step back, they can think more clearly. They then may be able to (or more precisely, be helped to) see connections between various complaints and the role they play in maintaining and even producing their own problems. Tracking involves seeing not only the connections between beliefs, but how these belief systems affect the clients on a daily basis in their actions and interactions (Shulman & Mosak, 1988).

Berne (1972) has remarked that it takes considerable effort to run out of gas in a car. He is correct. Think about what has to be done, and significantly, not done (overlooked) in order to run out of gas. He claims that he knows people who have lived a lifetime without ever running out of gas. He also knows others who seem to do it regularly. And that is his point. The old Hungarian proverb recommends, "If one person calls you a horse, laugh it off. If two people call you a horse, give it serious thought. If three people call you a horse, run out and get yourself a saddle." In other words, if an event is recurrent, you must be doing something to cause it. People arrange *unconsciously* to run out of gas—

it does not merely happen to them. It has to be arranged. It requires effort not to look at the gauge, to plan the trip so that too much distance is traveled before the tank empties, not to stop at the station to fill up when the gauge is noticed. Some of the core beliefs that may be held by such people are "I am an excitement seeker!" "I'm a risk taker," "Others should clean up after my mistakes," or "I'm exempt from life's responsibilities. The rules don't apply to me. Besides I rely on a Divine Providence."

These are just some of the possible connections that might be made from just one fact—regularly, or at least periodically, running out of gas. If the counselor can take the client through a typical day, it may be possible to track the effects of the belief system throughout. In another example, controllers may tie knots in their shoelaces in the morning, have a regularly planned breakfast at an exact time according to a preplanned schedule, know what outfit to wear because of the order in which the clothes are neatly hanging in the closet, and have the car and house keys systematically organized so that each is in the right order for maximum efficiency as they lock the door. They will have their papers in perfect…. The point is clear, and it is not yet even quarter past nine in the morning.

Much the same can be done with constellations or beliefs that generate lifestyles (Mosak, 1971). Clients are often amazed at the consistency of their patterns. Logical analysis of such patterns opens the door for change to take place, either through reappraisal of the goal or the methods of attaining the goal.* Locus of control is shifted, as well, as the clients perceive the role they play in generating their problems.

THE LOGICAL CORNER

Patients can paint themselves into a logical corner. Take the example of a young woman with suicidal preoccupations. Every morning when she arose, she placed a butcher knife on the

---

*Adler (1956) felt that the neurosis was an unconscious "arrangement of thinking, feeling, and behavior (including symptoms) which helped meet an unconscious goal of security." Greenburg (1966) embellishes this concept in his popular book *How to Make Yourself Miserable.*

kitchen table, and watched the knife all morning while she engaged in angry, despondent thoughts. At this session she challenged the therapist, initiating the following dialogue:

Patient: All right, if I didn't watch the knife, what should I be
             doing?
Therapist: I can't tell you what you should be doing, but there
             are certainly many things you could be doing.
Patient: Like what?
Therapist: Well, what are your friends doing this weekend?
Patient: They're all getting on a ski train to go skiing in Col-
             orado.
Therapist: Well, you could also go with them.
Patient: Yeah, and get killed on the slopes?

17

Dream Tactics

Since Freud (1950) first published his work on dream interpretation, psychotherapists have considered it an important tool in their work. Freud considered dreams to be "the royal road to the unconscious," and through careful analysis and interpretation, the analyst could understand various aspects of the patients' unconscious dynamics. Since Freud's work on dreams and the dream process, many other theorists have presented alternative views on the dynamics of dream life, most notably A. Adler (1956), K. Adler (1969), Bonime (1962), Boss (1958), Dreikurs (1944/1967b), Fromm (1951), Gold (1981), Jung (1959), and Shulman (1969). Where Freud saw the dream as a wish fulfillment, others, for example, Kurt Adler (1969) and French (1952), saw the dream as a problem-solving endeavor. With this approach, therapists do not primarily "look back" into childhood for an unresolved childhood conflict; they look "forward," toward upcoming events for which the patient is attempting to find a solution (Mosak, 1992). For them, the language of dreams is not disguised in an effort to conceal forbidden and repressed wishes from a watchful and potentially punitive superego (the censor). The dream language is an expression of the dreamers' idiosyncratic use of symbols that may or may not have universal, fixed meanings (Fromm, 1951). Without the necessity of communicating to others, a rich, metaphorical lexicon that will best serve the dreamers in their attempt to solve problems replaces the need for grammatical niceties and traditional constructions. The dream is a concise, powerful form of communicating with oneself. One other purpose of the dream is to generate a mood, to set the emotional tone for the day, for the dreamer (Adler, 1956). The emotions generated during the night, particularly those experienced closest to the time of awakening, are those that stay with the dreamer throughout the day, or at least at the beginning of the day.

As a tactic in counseling and psychotherapy, dreams can be used in many ways. They can tap into internal dialogue of the person. Personal use of symbols can be understood and deciphered. The idiosyncratic way the person solves problems can be observed and attended to, and the potential response a client may make to an upcoming challenge can be assessed as well. Dreams can be a point of departure for discussion even when they are not interpreted—such as, "What else in life frightens you?"

Unlike early recollections, dreams are not always indicative of clients' core belief systems. The latter are more situation-specific and deal with issues that are current. Recurrent dreams, however, may have more long-term, personality-style dynamics about them in that they represent the dreamers' repeated attempts to remain vigilant and address apparently repetitive challenges. Three specific tactics will be described.

HOW TO REMEMBER A DREAM

Before psychotherapists can use dreams in their clinical work, clients must bring them in. This sometimes made it difficult for the classical analyst because to ask for a dream was equivalent to asking for a gift. Later therapists have discarded this prohibition. Since, according to recent sleep laboratory findings, it has been concluded that everyone dreams every night, the issue becomes one of how clients can remember those dreams. Faraday (1972) has presented a useful approach, much of it similar to that of Dreikurs (personal communication). Faraday suggests that people keep a pen and paper or a recorder at bedside. Before going to sleep they are to tell themselves repeatedly that they will awaken from a dream that night. Keeping an alarm clock at bedside, they are to awaken themselves either two hours after going to sleep or at a time later in the typical sleep period, for example, two hours before normal awakening. Awakening should be done gradually because, as Faraday reports, being jolted too strongly into wakefulness can hamper the dream memory. Upon awakening to the alarm, they are to record the dream in as much detail as possible. They are not merely to use reminder cues in the belief that the details will be remembered in the morning, because the details will probably not be remembered then. If this procedure is followed, most clients will be able to bring in dreams.

DREAMING A PROBLEM

One can also ask clients to concentrate upon a particular problem or issue in their lives before going to bed. Provided that the client does not have a sleep disturbance that can potentially complicate the matter, one can utilize this tactic. Cartwright (1978) offers a detailed rationale for this tactic. When asked to think about issues shortly before sleeping, clients will have them fresh in mind when the process begins. In the morning, after having dreamt, clients may have a solution to their problems or, at least, a clarification of what is going on from their perspective.

A female client in her late twenties had questions about recurring nightmares, marital dissatisfaction, and dysthymia. She reported that she felt confused, anxious, and undecided about what was happening in her life and, specifically, what she wanted to do about her marriage. She was asked to think about these issues shortly before retiring at night. She did and came in for her session with the following dream:

> I am in a giant warehouse filled with huge boxcars. They are stacked all the way to the ceiling. I had stacked them there. I was quite proud of my work. All of a sudden, the floor beneath my feet began to shake and move up and down. The boxcars started to fall. I became panicked and ran out of the warehouse.

The clients' associations shed some light upon the dream and what was happening in her life. She associated the warehouse with her house. The boxcars represented all the effort and work that had gone into the family and her marriage. When asked about what she was thinking about before she went to sleep, she said that, of all of the issues she mulled over, whether or not to stay in her marriage was most prominent. The meaning of the dream became clear. She was expressing "good intentions"; that is, she was planning to leave her husband and children, but before she could bring herself to "run away," she had to shake things up a bit, create some commotion, and could then appear justified in her action. She laughed, and for the first time in her therapy, acknowledged that this had been exactly what she was thinking but had never verbalized to anyone, and she had barely admitted it to herself. On one level, she felt justified in her complaints against her family and yet, on another level, she somehow sensed that she was almost deliberately shaking things up lately in order to cause enough trouble, but hadn't known why. Now she knew it was done to justify her leaving. With the situation and her intentions clarified, therapeutic interventions were instituted.

GESTALT DREAM TACTICS

Perls (1970) and the Gestalt school of psychotherapy have introduced another dream tactic. He asked clients to assume the different parts/elements of their dreams. Interpretation, in the traditional, intellectual meaning of the word, is not as important as actually becoming that part of the dream and expressing the point of view of the dream from that perspective. It is a form of dream interpretation that is action-oriented. This tactic requires clients to use role-playing, role reversal, and many other psychodramatic techniques. For Perls, clients have failed to fully integrate certain aspects of their personality either through repression or projection, and by having them actually play the different elements of their dreams, they can reidentify with these out-of-touch aspects of themselves. For instance, a man who dreams that he is drowning in the sea and unable to reach a lifeboat just a few feet away would be asked to act the part of himself, the water he is swimming in, and the lifeboat. Playing these elements, he might be able to get in touch with parts of himself that he has not understood, resolve past issues, and better prepare himself to move ahead with his life. Holistic psycho-therapists would not find this method congenial.

From a slightly modified but congruent point of view, such a tactic could be conceptualized as a way of asking clients to as-sume another perspective upon their problems and the role that they play in maintaining them. As discussed in a number of dif-ferent sections of this book, clients quite often fail to see the con-nection between events in their lives and their own apperceptions of the events. By asking the client to role-play not only the swim-ming unsuccessfully but also the water and the boat, he may be able to obtain better understanding of himself and how he gen-erated and maintained his situation.

18

Humor

Adler (1956) considered humor, and jokes specifically, important in the therapeutic encounter because he liked to keep the therapy light. Mosak (1987a), Mosak and Maniacci (1993), and O'Connell (1975b) have written extensively on the use of humor from the perspective of Adlerian theory, as have Kuhlmann (1984) and Mindess (1971) from other points of view. Adler (1956), Ansbacher (1965), and Dreikurs (1973) make the distinction between common sense and private logic. Common sense is that which the general population shares; it is readily communicated and consensually validated. Private logic is that which the person cannot consensually express; it is normally not open to consensual validation and comprises the idiosyncratic aspects of the person's personality—in Adlerian terms, the style of life. Private logic is formed out of experiences the individual has during development. If enough experience is gained, the person is encouraged to do many things and explore creatively. The private logic will be flexible and, in general, in tune with common sense. Adler (1956) points out that "neurosis and the joke have similar characteristics. While the listener uses a normal frame of reference, the one who tells the joke suddenly introduces a new frame of reference...[which] shows the matter in an entirely new light" (p. 252). The joke can touch upon the new "frame of reference" (the private logic) and bring it into focus.

Mosak (1987a) delineates five major uses of humor in psychotherapy.

1. Humor can be beneficial in building the therapeutic relationship or any relationship for that matter. Humor and laughter bind people together, provided they all enjoy the same kind of humor.
2. Humor can be used as an aid in diagnosis. Certain lifestyle types such as martyrs, controllers, and feeling avoiders tend to have a poor sense of humor, while excitement seekers tend to gravitate and create humorous situations much of the time. There is also variability in sensitivity to humor in persons with medical diagnosis.
3. Humor can be a pointed form of interpretation. Interpretations can be less threatening and more memorable when couched in humor. For example, while Wolpe (1958) does not list humor as "a response antagonistic to anxiety" (p. 71), it certainly can be used for reciprocal inhibition.
4. Humor can be especially useful in turning the client around. Nothing ruins a good depression like a smile does. It is also difficult to be anxious and to laugh simultaneously, "nervous laughter" being a notable exception. Where many of the clients in therapy seek distance from others (Horney, 1950), humor invites movement toward others.
5. Humor can aid the therapist in making decisions about termination. If the client has gained a sense of humor about things, particularly his or her past situation, then termination may be near.

Humor is not for everybody. That statement applies not only to clients but to clinicians as well. If a therapist is comfortable with humor, she or he might use it. If not, other tactics would be preferable (Mosak, 1987a).

THE WITCHES' CIRCLE

Wolfe (1932) devised this tactic to practice involvement with other people. He prescribed the following to the patient:

Find a good story and tell it to at least one person during the day. If the first person you tell the story to does not laugh, continue until you have made someone laugh. If you cannot find anyone to laugh at your stories, there is a danger that your sense of humor is perverted. Get someone to tell you a story that he thinks is amusing. Tell this story to someone else until you have established a communal bond of good humor. Continue with this prescription until you have experienced the reward of citizenship in the republic of laughter. (pp. 187–188)

TWISTED ADAGES

Like some of the tactic of creating images, twisted adages can prompt clients to stop and think about what they are doing, thereby interrupting their typical transactions and patterns. Mosak (1987a) presents some examples of such adages. As we have already noted, Krausz (personal communication) would inform patients who want to be cured yesterday, "He who is impatient remains a patient." The late movie producer Sam Goldwyn is noted for his warning, "Anyone who goes to see a psychiatrist ought to have his head examined." Patients also create these adages. An "always play it safe" patient lamented to her therapist that her credo was "Nothing ventured, nothing lost!" while a man in marital therapy described his home situation in these terms: "A man's home is his hassle." Creative patients and therapists will create their own.

JOKES

Using jokes to illustrate points is useful, and having clients tell jokes can be even more so. Clients who are depressed can be instructed to tell the therapist or group a joke. The atmosphere of the session can change dramatically even after one joke on the part of the client. The aim is to interrupt the client's "negative nonsense" (O'Connell, 1975b). The latter are the negative, self-defeating thoughts and preoccupations that interfere with the engagement in meaningful activities. Joke telling asks clients to admit that the focus of their attention can be on more than with what is wrong. It can also instill hope—things can't be all that bad if they can still joke and laugh.

RATIONAL SONGS

Ellis (1997b) introduced and wrote several rational humorous songs that "are designed to repetitively go around and around in your patients' heads, like advertising jingles that they hear over radio and TV stations, and thereby to have their messages sink in and influence the person who sings them or internally 'hears' them" (p. 147).

19

Illustrative Tactics

Illustrative tactics embrace a wide variety of techniques—parables and fables, stories, true examples, and examples from literature, the movies and television. They can be used to make a point, to reinforce a point already made, to avoid confrontation, and to meet the client's request, "I don't understand. Give me an example of that."

PARABLES AND FABLES

To accomplish the aims of illustration, some therapists resort to parables and fables. The richest sources for the former are the Hebrew and Christian Bibles as well as the Chasidic masters (Buber, 1987).* *Aesop's Fables* (1968) represents the best source for fables among English-speaking people; La Fontaine (1988) is well known in other parts of the world. Among Aesop's fables, one of the most popular ones for therapeutic use is the Fox and the Grapes.

> A hungry fox saw some bunches of grapes hanging from a vine high up in the air. He tried his best to reach them by jumping as high as he could into the air. Unfortunately, they were beyond his

*In the Jewish Bible, parables can be found in II Samuel, I Kings, Isaiah, and Ezekiel. In the Christian Bible, 31 parables appear in the various books.

reach, so he gave up, walked away with dignity and unconcern, and remarked, "Those grapes are probably sour anyway."

This fable illustrates how the pride system is preserved. Unable to admit deficiency or defeat, the fox preserved his pride by denying that he even wanted the grapes. Whenever one hears a patient petulantly remarking, "I don't care," he or she probably cares too much to admit it.

"The Miller, His Son and the Ass," told to the pleaser, seeks to impress the pleaser with the moral, "He who tries to please everyone, pleases no one" or as one therapist paraphrases it for his patients, "he who tries to please everyone winds up losing his ass." The story is as follows:

A miller and his young son were taking their ass to the marketplace to sell him. On the road they met a group of giggling girls who exclaimed, "Did you ever see fools like that? They walk when they could be riding!" The miller thought that that made sense so he placed his son on the ass while he walked at the side. Soon they met some of his old friends who greeted them and said, "Why do you spoil that son of yours, letting him ride while you walk? Make him walk. It'll do him good!" The miller took their advice and took his son's place on the ass while the boy walked. They hadn't gone very far when they met a group of women and children who said, "What a selfish old man! He rides comfortably but lets his poor young son try to keep up as best as he can." So he got his son up on the ass with him. Then they met some travellers who asked whether the ass was his or hired for the occasion. He replied that it was his and he was taking it to the market to sell. They said, "With a load like that the poor animal will be so tired when he gets to market that no one will want to buy him. You'd better carry him!" "We'll do anything to please," said the miller, and they both got off, tied the ass's legs together, tied him to a pole and carried him to the marketplace. People ran out to laugh at this ridiculous sight, and teased the miller and son mercilessly. Some people even called them lunatics. By this time they had reached a bridge over a river, and the ass, frightened by this situation, kicked and broke the ropes with which he was bound, fell into the river, and drowned. The poor miller returned home, having learned that in attempting to please everyone, he had succeeded in pleasing no one, and had lost his ass too.

Another fable tells of the two frogs that fell into a churn of milk. The pessimistic frog gave up, sank to the bottom and drowned. The more optimistic frog, determined to survive, began to paddle. In doing so, he churned the milk into butter, and there he was on dry land. As Pancner (1978) points out, various therapists have their favorite fables for therapeutic illumination.

Some therapists create their own fables when the more traditional ones do not make the point they wish to make. Beecher (personal communication) told the following one:

> Ignoring the importuning and warnings of the flock, a sparrow remained behind in Manhattan. Because he was having so much fun, he was reluctant to leave with the flock for the south. However, he soon realized that he could wait no longer and started to fly south. On his way, he hit an ice storm and his wings frosted up, and he plummeted to the ground. Knowing he was now going to die, he berated himself for his foolhardiness for waiting too long and not listening to his friends. As he resigned himself to imminent death, a cow came by and dropped dung on him. The warmth defrosted his wings and he even had himself a little lunch. Knowing now that he had been spared at the last moment, he burst out in a song of praise to the Lord. Just then a cat passed by, and hearing the sparrow's song, shoveled the dung aside and promptly gobbled up the sparrow. There are three morals to this story:
>
> 1. Not everyone who shits on you is your enemy.
> 2. Not everyone who takes shit off you is your friend.
> 3. If you're full of shit, keep you mouth shut.

MYTHS

Psychoanalysts and analytical psychologists, especially, have displayed a fondness for the use of myths. At the therapist's disposal are such myths as Oedipus, Electra, Sisyphus, and Hercules and the Augean stables. Therapists who are unfamiliar with myths might profitably consult *Bulfinch's Mythology* (1979).

BIBLE STORIES

Many Bible stories lend themselves to use in psychotherapy—for example, various sibling rivalry stories (Sicher, 1950/1991), the bipolar King Saul and the later-to-be King David (the first music therapist), David and Goliath, Jacob wrestling with the "angel," and Lot's wife. In addition to Bible stories, there are biblical statements that can be utilized. An obsessive patient who saw devils around him, and therefore had to protect himself with rituals, was taught to use the counter, "Into Thy hands I commend my spirit" (Psalm 31). Supportive therapists may encourage the patient to "Be strong and of good courage" (*Deuteronomy* 31:23).

20

Multiple Psychotherapy

Although the use of two therapists with one patient had been long in use for specific purposes, it was not until Dreikurs that multiple psychotherapy or cotherapy was employed as a routine method in therapy (Dreikurs, Shulman, & Mosak, 1984). Multiple therapy can be used in individual, group, marriage, or family therapy. It can be used with therapists of the same or different sexes, with therapists with different degrees of experience—such as a supervisor and trainee, and with therapists with reasonably consonant theoretical-philosophical outlooks. A classically trained psychoanalyst and a client-centered therapist would not make good partners.

Some of the benefits to the patient are the following:

1. It prevents the patient from feeling misunderstood or abused by the therapist.
2. Patients get a more realistic perception of their therapists. This is a benefit only for those therapists whose orientations do not rely upon the transference.
3. The patient benefits from learning from two persons, from adapting to two personalities, from two styles of interaction. The constant interjection of fresh viewpoints keeps the therapy from bogging down.
4. Multiple psychotherapy permits the patient to be both spectator and participant. She or he can be the subject of discussion and simultaneously the "objective" viewer of the proceedings.

5. In individual therapy, if the therapist and patient do not "hit it off" or reach an impasse, the patient might terminate therapy entirely. In multiple therapy, the chances of this occurring are diminished, and the patient does not have to start over again. The cotherapist can be "appealed to" as consultant or buffer to analyze the problem, or the patient can be transferred to the cotherapist who now serves as the principal therapist.
6. The method does not foster the patient's dependence upon a single person. Both therapists can work to forestall such patient attempts.
7. Illness or the vacation of one of the therapists does not place the patient in the position of being without support or a therapist; the cotherapist merely takes over. Attachment is to therapy rather than to the therapist.
8. Finally, the therapists' interactions become a model for the patient. The patient can observe how cooperative, adult interactions are managed and how disagreement and divergent views can be successfully handled.

For the therapist, some of the advantages may be the following:

1. First, and foremost, constant consultation is provided. This reduces the possibility of therapist bias, therapist error, and feelings of impotence, and produces support for the therapist.* Haley (1987) uses a similar form of in vivo supervision.
2. With two therapists, the chances of falling into therapeutic traps decrease. No matter how thorough the therapist's "didactic" analysis (assuming the therapist has undergone one), the therapist's biases, convictions, and "countertransferences" never completely vanish. Whenever the therapist becomes caught up with the patient, the cotherapist can intervene.
3. Therapists are given the opportunity to play different roles in relation to the patient.
4. Two therapists can help with the resistance by, for example, "double-teaming" the patient.
5. The therapist can take time off for illness, vacation, and personal affairs.

*At the Adler School of Professional Psychology in Chicago, therapists are trained in this manner, and many graduates continue to use this form of therapy after graduation.

6. One therapist can adopt the participant role while the other may be observer or participant-observer. This may afford the consultant an opportunity to understand what is going on, to assess why therapy may be in a rut or at an impasse, and to extract the primary therapist from some undesirable position.

Multiple psychotherapy as practiced by Dreikurs, Shulman, and Mosak (1984) has one therapist assume the consultant role, with the other assuming the primary role. These roles may be reversed when therapeutic considerations demand it. Double sessions are held every three to four meetings, with the consultant attending and actively participating. In group, marriage, and family therapy, both may attend each session.

While some may counter that multiple psychotherapy is not cost-effective, the truth is that the overall length of therapy will usually be abbreviated by the use of two therapists (Dreikurs, Shulman, & Mosak, 1984).

DISCUSSING THE CLIENT

Discussing the client in front of the client can be intriguing. A resistant, unmotivated individual can usually be "stirred up" and challenged. The client can be the observer of his or her own therapy. The client is encouraged to "jump in" at any time and correct, change, argue, agree, elaborate, or modify anything that is said.

This tactic is valuable in providing what is known as a sense of decentering (Beck, 1976). Clients can "step back" from their problems and take a somewhat more objective stance. They can hear their private logic discussed. What was once unspoken or only "dimly envisioned" can be put into words and brought into awareness. "I don't know, do you think he's out to prove how tough he is?" asks one therapist. "Well, that could be one reason, but I have another guess. I think he's very afraid that we might find out just how much of a failure he thinks he is." The client is almost invariably "glued" to the therapists' conversation throughout.

Another aspect of discussing the client is that the therapists can check out and modify their own ideas about the therapeutic process. This process resembles the method of successive approximation in mathematics. Not only is such a process useful in supervision, it can serve to clarify the client's conceptions about what is transpiring in therapy. "So you two see me as being more scared than angry, and that I use my anger to bluff my way through situations I don't think I can handle? You might be right." Hearing two people discuss something about you can be exceedingly hard to resist—one's attention is immediately drawn to them.

Interpretations can be "dramatically heightened" as well, thus giving more weight and significance. "I think I know why they do that to each other," the cotherapist can remark, "but I don't know if I should say it." "Oh, go on. I'm sure I can take it," can be the response. "Well, it's been such a big secret for so long that I wonder if they'll try to downplay it once we give it away." "Yeah, but it has to be said," the other therapist can reply.

Occasionally a patient will object that she or he hates being treated as an "object." In those instances, this tactic should be avoided.

DISAGREEING IN FRONT OF THE PATIENT

Therapists can intentionally disagree, even debate, in front of a client. This may serve many purposes. First, it is an excellent modeling technique. Clients can actually observe that to disagree is not necessarily something bad, that people can disagree respectfully, and that conflicts can be resolved peacefully without a sense of defeat or loss. Second, it can create therapeutic alignment. The primary therapist and client can "side together" against the consultant, thus strengthening the relationship and reinforcing the acceptance of therapeutic issues. Third, clients can be brought into the debate. They can then be placed in the position of explaining and "defending" their actions or intentions on a new level. "No, not really. It's not that I was tired. I was trying to get even. You're right." Fourth, a client who was previously "resistant," perhaps uncooperatively silent, may interpose, "You're both wrong. I'll show you that I'm not that bad," or "You two only have part of it, but there's a part you don't know about." And fifth, clients can gain a sense of encouragement from the process. For many, hearing two people discuss and debate them is the most important they have felt in years, maybe even their lives. They can begin to believe that they do matter to someone and that others do care and are concerned.

Disagreement can also be instructive to the pleaser (Hart, 1977; Mosak, 1971). Pleasers often can't understand what's wrong with being a pleaser. They confuse *wanting* to please with *having* to please. We can illustrate the pleaser's difficulties by disagreeing and then asking clients which therapist they agree with. They immediately, although painfully, see the major problem in trying to be universally pleasing.

ACTING NAIVE

Another ploy is to have one therapist act naive at certain points. "I don't understand," one therapist can say. "Why would someone want to put himself through such pain and discomfort just at the thought of going out in public?" Such a query provides an opening for an interpretation from the other therapist which superficially is directed to the first therapist but, in reality, is presenting what may be a rather touchy issue to the client.

Acting naive can be a way of having the client open up and discuss certain topics—in this case, to ostensibly explain things to the other therapist. "You see," says the client, "what he's talking about is how I set people up. He feels that I strike out at others before they get a chance to strike out at me." Client are then in a position to assume more responsibility for their actions and for therapy.

BEING INTENTIONALLY WRONG

The converse of acting naive, and a variation of disagreeing, is to have one therapist be "wrong." If one is wrong and argues the point strongly, the other therapist can enlist the aid of the client in setting the first therapist "straight."

Therapist 1: I think he does it because he just don't care anymore.

Therapist 2: I don't know. If he didn't care, surely there would be easier ways of showing it.

T1:   Look at his body language. That's what he seems to be telling everyone.

T2:   Bob, is that true? I can't believe that you just don't care anymore.

C: No, I *do* care!

T1:   I'm not sure I believe that. My impression is that you're trying to push everyone away.

T2:   To the contrary. He's trying to get them to take care of him. How can he do that if he's pushing them away? Right, Bob?

C: Well, in a way, yeah. I'm almost ashamed to admit it, but yeah. You're wrong. It's not that I don't care. It's just that...."

With the "devil's advocate" not pushing too forcefully, and if it is used selectively, being intentionally wrong may hasten therapeutic progress.

Conclusion

Tactics, in counseling or psychotherapy, are tools professionals use to help people. In summary, let us examine where we have been and what we have stated.

Whereas a strategy tells you what the overall goal of the system of psychotherapy or counseling is, a technique tells you how to arrive at that goal. For example, in classical psychoanalysis, the overall strategy is to make the unconscious conscious—that is, to provide insight. Some of the common techniques are free association, dream interpretation, and analysis of the transference. In structural family therapy, the overall strategy is to rebalance the system and reestablish the appropriate hierarchical structure. Some of the common techniques are joining, enacting, and establishing boundaries.

Tactics are the application of techniques to a particular situation. For example, when and how should you interpret a dream? When and how should you establish a boundary? Imagine the following conversation in a supervisory session: A student asks, "What do I do when my client cries?" The supervisor answers by saying, "Analyze the transference." The student asked a tactical question, and the supervisor gave a technical answer. They were operating at cross-purposes, and neither may feel satisfied with the outcome. Or another instance: The student asks, "What are some ways I can put the parents back in charge?" and the supervisor responds by saying, "By reestablishing the appropriate family structure." The student asked a tactical question, and the supervisor gave a strategic response. Once again, they were at cross-purposes.

Supervision and teaching in counseling and psychotherapy are facilitated when those doing the supervision or teaching strive to align goals with the goals of those being supervised or those learning the counseling or psychotherapy. In other words, the same process of goal alignment that is needed between client and therapist is needed between supervisor and student. This book is an attempt to delineate tactics—that is, techniques that are situation-specific and answer the question, "What do I do when...?"

Tactics in Counseling and Psychotherapy is not designed to replace books that teach strategy. It cannot substitute for a thorough grounding in assessment, theory, and good, old-fashioned experience. And, as we have repeatedly tried to emphasize, there is no substitute for knowing your clients. Clients are more than their "problems"; they are people—with diverse ethnic, religious, cultural, and developmental histories. They need to be understood as unique.

Finally, use only what you are comfortable with, yet do not be afraid to try something new. Having the courage to be imperfect and take a risk by trying some new tactics does not mean taking unnecessary risks or doing what is very uncomfortable for either you or your patients. We ask patients to risk, and try new behaviors, attitudes, and thoughts. We should be willing to have the flexibility that we ask of them.

We have provided a series of tactics that is neither exhaustive nor complete. We do not know if any such book could ever be "complete"—and maybe it should not be. Humans are creative: Perhaps that is their defining characteristic. When we use our creativity to grow, we attain wonderful heights. When, in spite of our creativity, we stay "stuck" and cause trouble for ourselves and others, the resulting pain and frustration can be intense. Do not be afraid to form your own tactics; go and learn others from supervisors, colleagues, peers—even clients, friends, plays, movies, and novels. *Use* your creativity. We hope this book will be helpful in your practice, but if it elicits your originality in coming up with more and "better" tactics, then we have done more than provide a text of tactics, we have helped stimulate your thinking and your own invention. Perhaps that is as much as anyone can ask.

References

Adler, A. (1927). A doctor remakes education. *Survey, 58*, 490–495.

Adler, A. (1956). *The individual psychology of Alfred Adler*. H. L. Ansbacher & R. R. Ansbacher (Eds.). New York: Harper & Row.

Adler, A. (1964a). *Problems of neurosis*. P. Mairet (Ed.). New York: Harper & Row. (Original work published 1929.)

Adler, A. (1964b). Technique of treatment. In H. L. Ansbacher & R. R. Ansbacher (Eds.), *Superiority and social interest* (pp. 191–201). New York: Norton. (Original work published 1932.)

Adler, K. A. (1961). Depression in the light of Individual Psychology. *Journal of Individual Psychology, 17*(1), 56–67.

Adler, K. A. (1969). Discussion. In M. Kramer (Ed.), *Dream psychology and the new biology of dreaming* (pp. 138–140). Springfield, IL: Charles C. Thomas.

Aesop. (1968). *Aesop's fables*. New York: F. Watts.

Angus, L., & Rennie, D. L. (1989). Envisioning the repreentational world: The client's experience of metaphoric expression in psychotherapy. *Psychotherapy, 26*(3), 372–379.

Ansbacher, H. L. (1965). *Sensus privatus versus sensus communis. Journal of Individual Psychology, 21*, 48–50.

Arlow, J. A. (1958). Truth or motivations? Toward a definition of psychoanalysis. *The Saturday Review, 14*, 55–56.

Ascher, L. M. (1989). *Therapeutic paradox*. New York: Guilford Press.

Bandura, A. (1977). *Social learning theory*. Englewood Cliffs, NJ: Prentice-Hall.

Bassin, A. (1975). Red, white, and blue poker chips: An A.A. behavior modification technique. *American Psychologist, 30*, 695–696.

Bateson, G., Jackson, D., Haley, J., & Weakland, J. (1956). Toward a theory of schizophrenia. *Behavioral Science, 1,* 251–264.

Beck, A. T. (1976). *Cognitive therapy and the emotional disorders.* New York: Meridian.

Bedrosian, R. C., & Beck, A. T. (1980). Principles of cognitive therapy. In M. J. Mahoney (Ed.), *Psychotherapy process* (pp. 127–152). New York: Plenum Press.

Beecher, W., & Beecher, M. (1971). *Beyond success and failure.* New York: Pocket Books. (Original work published 1966.)

Berne, E. (1964). *Games people play.* New York: Grove Press.

Berne, E. (1972). *What do you say after you say hello?* New York: Grove Press.

Bixler, R. H. (1949). Limits are therapy. *Journal of Consulting Psychology 13*(1), 1–11.

Boldt, R. (1994). *Lifestyle types and therapeutic resistance: An Adlerian model for prediction and intervention of characterological resistance in therapy.* Unpublished Psy.D. dissertation. Chicago: Adler School of Professional Psychology.

Bonime, W. (1962). *The clinical use of dreams.* New York: Basic Books.

Boss, M. (1958). *The analysis of dreams.* New York: Philosophical Library.

Brewer, D. H. (1976). *The induction and alteration of state depression; A comparative study.* Unpublished Ph.D. dissertation, University of Houston.

Brown, P. (1995). *The reliability and validity of "The Question" in the differential diagnosis of somatogenic and psychogenic disorders.* Unpublished Psy.D. dissertation. Chicago: Adler School of Professional Psychology.

Buber, M. (1987). *Tales of the Hasidim.* New York: Schocken.

Bugental, J. F. T., & Bugental, E. K. (1984). A fate worse than death: The fear of changing. *Psychotherapy, 21*(4), 543–549.

Bulfinch, T. (1979). *Bulfinch's mythology.* New York: Avenel.

Cartwright, R. D. (1978, December). Happy endings for our dreams. *Psychology Today,* 66–76.

Corsini, R. J. (1966). *Roleplaying in psychotherapy.* Chicago: Aldine.

Corsini, R. J. (1967). Let's invent a first aid kit for marriage. *Consultant* (Smith, Kline & French Laboratories), 7, 40.

Coué, E. (1922a). *The practice of autosuggestion.* New York: Doubleday.

Coué, E. (1922b). *Self mastery through conscious suggestion.* London: Allen & Unwin.

Coyne, J. C. (1984). Strategic therapy with depressed married persons: Initial agenda, themes, and interventions. *Journal of Marital and Family Therapy, 10,* 53–62.

Credner, L. (1936). Safeguards. *International Journal of Individual Psychology, 2*(3), 95–102.

Dinkmeyer, D. C., & Dreikurs, R. (1963). *Encouraging children to learn: The encouragement process.* Englewood Cliffs, NJ: Prentice-Hall.

Dinkmeyer, D. C., & McKay, G. D. (1973). *Raising a responsible child.* New York: Simon & Schuster.

Dreikurs, R. (1953). *Fundamentals of Adlerian psychology.* Chicago: Alfred Adler Institute.

Dreikurs, R. (1958). A reliable differential diagnosis of psychological or somatic disturbance. *International Record of Medicine, 171,* 238–242.

Dreikurs, R. (1962). Can you be sure the disease is functional? *Consultant* (Smith, Kline & French Laboratories).

Dreikurs, R. (1967a). *Psychodynamics, psychotherapy and counseling.* Chicago: Alfred Adler Institute.

Dreikurs, R. (1967b). The meaning of dreams. In R. Dreikurs, *Psychodynamics, psychotherapy and counseling* (pp. 219–229). Chicago: Alfred Adler Institute. (Original work published 1944.)

Dreikurs, R. (1973). The private logic. In H. H. Mosak (Ed.), *Alfred Adler: His influence on psychology today* (pp. 19–32). Park Ridge, NJ: Noyes Press.

Dreikurs, R. (1987). Are psychological schools of thought outdated? *Individual Psychology, 43,* 265–272. (Original work published 1960.)

Dreikurs, R., & Grey, L. (1968). *Logical consequences: A new approach to discipline.* New York: Meredith.

Dreikurs, R., & Mosak, H. H. (1966). The tasks of life. I. Adler's three tasks. *Individual Psychologist, 4,* 18–22.

Dreikurs, R., & Mosak, H. H. (1967). The tasks of life. II. The fourth task. *Individual Psychologist, 4 ,* 51–55.

Dreikurs, R., Shulman, B. H., & Mosak, H. H. (1984). *Multiple psychotherapy.* Chicago: Alfred Adler Institute.

Dreikurs, R., & Soltz, V. (1964). *Children: The challenge.* New York: Duell, Sloan & Pearce.

Dunlap, K. (1933). *Habits: Their making and unmaking.* New York: Liveright.

Ellis, A. (1972). 22 ways to stop putting yourself down. *Rational Living, 6*(2), 9–15.

Ellis, A. (1974). *Disputing irrational beliefs (DIBS).* New York: Institute for Rational Living.

Ellis, A. (1977a). *Anger: How to live with it and without it.* Secaucus, NJ: Citadel Press.

Ellis, A. (1977b). *A garland of rational songs.* New York: Institute for Rational Living.

Ellis, A., & Harper, R. A. (1975). *A new guide to rational living.* Hollywood, CA: Wilshire.

Fagan, J. (1975). ...And not a mere device. *Voices, 11*(1), 12–13.

Faraday, A. (1972). *Dream power.* New York: Berkeley Books.

Fast, J. (1970). *Body language.* New York: Pocket Books.

Ferenczi, S., & Rank, O. (1925). *The development of psychoanalysis.* New York: Nervous and Mental Disease Publishing Co.

Forer, B. R. (1969). The taboo against touching in psychotherapy. *Psychotherapy, 6,* 229–234.

Forgus, R., & Shulman, B. (1979). *Personality: A cognitive view.* Englewood Cliffs, NJ: Prentice-Hall.

Fox, R. E. (1980). The joy of inventing stories. *Voices, 15*(4), 39–45.

Frankl, V. E. (1963). *Man's search for meaning.* New York: Washington Square Press.

Frankl, V. E. (1967). Paradoxical intention. In H. Greenwald (Ed.), *Active psychotherapy* (pp. 337–352). New York: Atherton.

Frankl, V. E. (1968). *Psychotherapy and existentialism.* New York: Simon & Schuster.

Frankl, V. E. (1969). *The will to meaning.* New York: New American Library.

Frankl, V. E. (1985). Logos, paradox and the search for meaning. In M. J. Mahoney & A. Freeman (Eds.), *Cognition and psychotherapy* (pp. 259–275). New York: Plenum Press.

French, T. M. (1952). *The integration of behavior.* Vol. I. Chicago: University of Chicago Press.

Freud, S. (1937). Analysis terminable and interminable. In J. Strachey (Ed.), *Collected papers.* Vol. 5 (pp. 316–357). London: Hogarth.

Freud, S. (1950). *The interpretation of dreams.* New York: Modern Library.

Freud, S. (1958). The future prospects of psycho-analytic therapy. In J. Strachey (Ed.), *The standard edition of the complete works of Sigmund Freud.* Vol. II. London: Hogarth.

Fromm, E. (1951). *The forgotten language.* New York: Grove Press.

Fromm-Reichman, F. (1950). *Principles of intensive psychotherapy.* Chicago: University of Chicago Press.

Gendlin, E. (1981). *Focusing.* New York: Bantam Books.

Gold, L. (1981). Life style and dreams. In L. Baruth & D. Eckstein (Eds.), *Life style: Theory, practice and research* (2nd ed.) (pp. 24–30). Dubuque, IA: Kendall/Hunt.

Gordon, D. (1978). *Therapeutic metaphors.* Cupertino, CA: Meta Publications.

Gordon, T. (1970). *Parent effectiveness training.* New York: P. H. Wyden.

Greenberg, L. S. (1979). Resolving splits: Use of the two chair technique. *Psychotherapy, 16*(3), 316–324.

Greenburg, D. (1966). *How to make yourself miserable.* New York: Random House.

Greenspoon, J. (1955). The reinforcing effect of two spoken sounds on the frequency of two responses. *American Journal of Psychology, 68,* 409–416.

Gushurst, R. S. (1978, May). *Treating the severe obsessive-compulsive.* Paper presented at the meeting of the North American Society of Adlerian Psychology, Washington, DC.

Guthrie, R. D. (1977). *Body hot spots.* New York: Pocket Books.

Haley, J. (1963). *Strategies of psychotherapy.* New York: Grune & Stratton.

Haley, J. (1987). *Problem-solving therapy* (2nd ed.). San Francisco: Jossey-Bass.

Harlow, H. F. (1958). The nature of love. *American Psychologist, 13,* 673–685.

Harris, S. J. (1977, April 28). Most are vain; few conceited. *Chicago Daily News.*

Hart, J. L. (1977). Perils of the pleaser. In J. P. Madden (Ed.), *Loneliness* (pp. 41–55). Whitinsville, MA: Affirmation Books.

Hayman, M. (1942). Two minute clinical test for measurement of intellectual impairment in psychiatric disorders. *Archives of Neurology and Psychiatry, 47,* 454–464.

Hertz, J. (Ed.) (1958). *Sayings of the Fathers.* New York: Behrman.

Hoffman, E. (1994). *The drive for self: Alfred Adler and the founding of Individual Psychology.* Reading, MA: Addison-Wesley.

Horney, K. (1950). *Neurosis and human growth.* New York: Norton.

Horvat, A. (1937). Concerning stagefright. *International Journal of Individual Psychology, 3*(4), 50–355.

Jung, C. G. (1959). *The collected works.* Vol. 8. Princeton, NJ: Princeton University Press.

Kershaw-Bellemare, R., & Mosak, H. H. (1993). Adult Children of Alcoholics: An Adlerian perspective. *Journal of Alcohol and Drug Education, 38*(3), 105–119.

Kopp, R. R. (1995). *Metaphor therapy.* New York: Brunner/Mazel.

Kopp, R. R., & Kivel, C. (1990). Traps and escapes: An Adlerian approach to understanding resistance and resolving defenses in psychotherapy. *Individual Psychology, 46*(2), 139–147.

Krausz, E. O. (1935). The pessimistic attitude. *International Journal of Individual Psychology, 1*(3), 86–89.

Krausz, E. O. (1959). The homeostatic function of dreams. *Individual Psychology Newsletter, 9,* 48.

Kuhlmann, T. L. (1984). *Humor and psychotherapy.* Homewood, IL: Dow Jones-Irwin.

Künkel, F. (1972). *Das Wir: Die Grundbegriffe der Wir-Psychologie* [The We: Principles of We-Psychology]. Schwerin-Mecklinberg: Bahn. (Original work published 1939.)

La Fontaine, J. de (1988). *The complete fables of Jean de la Fontaine*. Evanston, IL: Northwestern University Press.

Lazarsfeld, S. (1966). Dare to be less than perfect. *Journal of Individual Psychology, 22*, 163–165.

Lecky, P. (1969). *Self-consistency*. New York: Doubleday Anchor Books. (Original work published 1945.)

Lenrow, P. B. (1966). Use of metaphor in facilitating constructive behavior change. *Psychotherapy, 3*, 145–148.

Lewin, K. (1937). Psychoanalysis and topological psychology. *Bulletin of the Menninger Clinic, 1*, 202–212.

Losoncy, L. E. (1977). *Turning people on: How to be an encouraging person*. Englewood Cliffs, NJ: Prentice-Hall.

Low, A. A. (1952). *Mental health through will training*. Boston: Christopher.

Mahoney, M. J. (1980). Psychotherapy and the structure of personal revolutions. In M. J. Mahoney (Ed.), *Psychotherapy process* (pp. 157–180). New York: Plenum Press.

Maimonides (1982). Letter to the Jews of Marseilles in 1194. In L. D. Stitskin (Ed.), *Letters of Maimonides*. New York: Yeshiva University Press.

Manaster, G. J., & Corsini, R. J. (1982). *Individual Psychology*. Itasca, IL: F. E. Peacock.

Maniacci, M. P. (1988). Language skills group: A psychoeducational group treatment approach. *Individual Psychology, 44*, 129–137.

Maniacci, M. P. (1991). Guidelines for developing social interest with clients in psychiatric day hospitals. *Individual Psychology, 47*, 177–178.

McMullin, R. C. (1986). *Handbook of cognitive therapy techniques*. New York: W. W. Norton.

Menninger, K. (1958). *Theory of psychoanalytic technique*. New York: Basic Books.

Merton, R. K. (1948). The self-fulfilling prophecy. *Antioch Review, 8*, 193–210.

Mindess, H. (1971). *Laughter and liberation*. Los Angeles, CA: Nash.

Mintz, E. (1969a). On the rationale of touch in psychotherapy. *Psychotherapy, 6*(4), 232–234.

Mintz, E. (1969b). Touch and the psychoanalytic tradition. *Psychoanalytic Review, 56*(3), 365–376.

Montagu, A. (1955). *The direction of human development*. New York: Harper.

Mosak, H. H. (1950). *Evaluation in psychotherapy: A study of some current measures*. Unpublished Ph.D. dissertation, University of Chicago.

Mosak, H. H. (1967). Subjective criteria of normality. *Psychotherapy, 4*(4), 159–161. Also in L. R. Alman & D. T. Jaffe (Eds.), *Readings in abnormal psychology* (pp. 11–12). New York: Harper & Row, 1976.

Mosak, H. H. (1971). Lifestyle. In A. Nikelly (Ed.), *Techniques for behavior change* (pp. 77–81). Springfield, IL: Charles C. Thomas.

Mosak, H. H. (1973). The controller: A social interpretation of the anal character. In H. H. Mosak (Ed.), *Alfred Adler: His influence on psychology today* (pp. 43–52). Park Ridge, NJ: Noyes Press.

Mosak, H. H. (1977). Does a "TMJ" personality exist? In H. Gelb (Ed.), *Clinical management of head, neck and TMJ pain and dysfunction* (pp. 195–205). Philadelphia: W. B. Saunders.

Mosak, H. H. (1978, May). *The assumptive universe of the paranoid patient.* Paper presented at the meeting of the North American Society of Adlerian Psychology, Washington, DC.

Mosak, H. H. (1979). The case of Bill [Film]. (Available from Adler School of Professional Psychology, 65 E. Wacker Place, Chicago, IL 60601.)

Mosak, H. H. (1985). Interrupting a depression: The pushbutton technique. *Individual Psychology, 41*(2), 210–214.

Mosak, H. H. (1987a). *Ha ha and aha: The role of humor in psychotherapy.* Muncie, IN: Accelerated Development.

Mosak, H. H. (1987b). Religious allusions in psychotherapy. *Individual Psychology, 43*(4), 496–501.

Mosak, H. H. (1990). For whoever believeth in it shall have everlasting life. In J. K. Zeig & W. M. Munion (Eds.), *What is psychotherapy?* (pp. 24–28). San Francisco: Jossey-Bass.

Mosak, H. H. (1991). "I don't have social interest:" Social interest as construct. *Individual Psychology, 47,* 309–320.

Mosak, H. H. (1992). The "traffic cop" function of dreams and early recollections. *Individual Psychology, 48,* 319–323.

Mosak, H. H. (1995). Adlerian psychotherapy. In R. J. Corsini & D. Wedding (Eds.), *Current psychotherapies* (pp. 51–94). Itasca, IL: F. E. Peacock.

Mosak, H. H., & Dreikurs, R. (1967). The life tasks. III. The fifth life task. *Individual Psychologist, 5,* 16–22.

Mosak, H. H., & Gushurst, R. S. (1971). What patients say and what they mean. *American Journal of Psychotherapy, 25*(3), 428–436.

Mosak, H. H., & Gushurst, R. S. (1972). Some therapeutic uses of psychologic testing. *American Journal of Psychotherapy, 26*(4), 539–546.

Mosak, H. H., & LeFevre, C. (1976). The resolution of "intrapersonal" conflict. *Individual Psychology, 32*(1), 19–26.

Mosak, H. H., & Maniacci, M. P. (1993). An "Adlerian" approach to humor and psychotherapy. In W. F. Fry, Jr. & W. S. Salameh (Eds.),

Advances in humor and psychotherapy (pp. 1–18). Sarasota, FL: Professional Resources Press.

Mosak, H. H., & Maniacci, M. P. (1995). The case of Roger. In D. Wedding & R. J. Corsini (Eds.), *Case studies in psychotherapy* (2nd ed.) (pp. 23–49). Itasca, IL: F. E. Peacock.

Mosak, H. H., & Phillips, K. S. (1980). *Demons, germs and values*. Chicago: Alfred Adler Institute.

Mosak, H. H., & Schneider, S. (1977). Masculine protest, penis envy, women's liberation and sexual equality. *Journal of Individual Psychology, 33*(2), 193–202.

Mosak, H. H., Shulman, B. H. (1966). *The neuroses: A syllabus*. Chicago: Alfred Adler Institute.

Mosak, H. H., & Shulman, B. H. (1974). *Individual psychotherapy: A syllabus* (rev. ed.). Chicago: Alfred Adler Institute.

Mosak, H. H., & Shulman, B. H. (1977). *Clinical assessment: A syllabus*. Chicago: Alfred Adler Institute.

Mozdzierz, G. J., Macchitelli, F. J., & Lisiecki, J. (1976). The paradox in psychotherapy: An Adlerian perspective. *Journal of Individual Psychology, 32*(2), 169–183.

Munroe, R. L. (1955). *Schools of psychoanalytic thought*. New York: Dryden Press.

Neuer, A. (1936). Courage and discouragement. *International Journal of Individual Psychology, 2*(2), 30–50.

Nierenberg, G. I., & Calero, H. H. (1971). *How to read a person like a book*. New York: Pocket Books.

Nikelly, A. G., & O'Connell, W. E. (1971). Action-oriented methods. In A. G. Nikelly (Ed.), *Techniques for behavior change* (pp. 85–90). Springfield, IL: Charles C. Thomas.

O'Connell, W. E. (1975a) *Action therapy and Adlerian theory*. Chicago: Alfred Adler Institute.

O'Connell, W. E. (1975b). The humorous attitude: Research and clinical beginnings. In W. E. O'Connell, *Action therapy and Adlerian theory* (pp. 183–197). Chicago: Alfred Adler Institute.

O'Connell, W. E., & Brewer, D. (1971). The value of role reversal in psychodrama and action therapy. *Handbook of International Sociometry, 6,* 98–104.

Omer, H. (1981). Paradoxical treatments: A unified concept. *Psychotherapy, 18,* 320–324.

Pancner, K. R. (1978). The use of parables and fables in Adlerian psychotherapy. *Individual Psychologist, 15*(4), 19–29.

Perls, F. S. (1970). Dream seminars. In F. Fagan & I. L. Shepard (Eds.), *Life techniques in Gestalt therapy* (pp. 165–199). Evanston, IL: Harper & Row.

Perman, S. (1975). Encouragement techniques. *Individual Psychologist, 11*(2), 13–18.

Pew, M. L., & Pew, W. L. (1972). Adlerian marriage counseling. *Journal of Individual Psychology, 28,* 192–202.

Phillips, C. E., & Corsini, R. J. (1982). *Give in—or give up.* Chicago: Nelson-Hall.

Raimy, V. (1975). *Misunderstandings of the self.* San Francisco: Jossey-Bass.

Reik, T. (1948). *Listening with the third ear.* New York: Grove Press.

Resnick, R. W. (1970). Chicken soup is poison. *Voices, 6*(2), 75–78.

Rogers, C. (1951). *Client-centered therapy.* Boston: Houghton Mifflin.

Rogers, C. R. (1957). The necessary and sufficient conditions of therapeutic personality change. *Journal of Consulting Psychology, 21,* 95–103.

Rogers, C. R. (1986). Client-centered therapy. In I. L. Kutash & A. Wolf (Eds.), *Psychotherapist's casebook: Therapy and technique in practice* (pp. 197–208). San Francisco: Jossey-Bass.

Rokeach, M. (1964). *The three Christs of Ypsilanti.* New York: Knopf.

Rosenthal, H. (1959). The final dream: A criterion for the termination of therapy. In K. A. Adler & D. Deutsch (Eds.), *Essays in Individual Psychology* (pp. 400–409). New York: Grove Press.

Rosenthal, V. (1975). Holding: A way through the looking glass? *Voices, 11*(1), 2–7.

Sherman, R., & Fredman, N. (1986). *Handbook of structured techniques in marriage and family therapy.* New York: Brunner/Mazel.

Shlien, J. M., Mosak, H. H., & Dreikurs, R. (1962). Effect of time limits: A comparison of two psychotherapies. *Journal of Counseling Psychology, 9,* 31–34.

Shoobs, N. E. (1946). The application of Individual Psychology through psychodramatics. *Individual Psychology Bulletin, 5,* 3–21.

Shulman, B. H. (1969). The Adlerian theory of dreams. In M. Kramer (Ed.), *Dream psychology and the new biology of dreaming* (pp. 117–140). Springfield, IL: Charles C. Thomas.

Shulman, B. H. (1973). *Contributions to Individual Psychology.* Chicago: Alfred Adler Institute. (Original work published 1964.)

Shulman, B. H. (1985). Cognitive therapy and the Individual Psychology of Alfred Adler. In M. J. Mahoney & A. Freeman (Eds.), *Cognition and psychotherapy* (pp. 243–258). New York: Plenum Press.

Shulman, B. H., & Mosak, H. H. (1967). Various purposes of symptoms. *Journal of Individual Psychology, 23,* 79–87.

Shulman, B. H., & Mosak, H. H. (1988). *A manual for life style assessment.* Muncie, IN: Accelerated Development.

Sicher, L. (1991). The family constellation (In the Old Testament). In A. Davidson (Ed.), *The collected works of Lydia Sicher* (pp. 476–504). Ft. Bragg, CA: QED Press. (Original work published 1950.)

Starr, A. (1977). *Rehearsal for living: Psychodrama.* Chicago: Nelson-Hall.

Steinbeck, J. (1937). *Of mice and men.* New York: Modern Library.

Steiner, C. (1974). *Scripts people live.* New York: Grove Press.

Stotland, E. (1969). *The psychology of hope.* San Francisco: Jossey-Bass.

Strub, R. L., & Black, F. W. (1993). *The mental status examination in neurology* (3rd ed.). Philadelphia: F. A. Davis.

Sturm, T. (1926). *Immensee.* New York: Irvington.

Szasz, T. S. (1965). *The ethics of psychoanalysis.* New York: Basic Books.

Taft, J. 1973). *The dynamics of therapy in a controlled relationship.* Gloucester, MA: Peter Smith. (Original work published 1933.)

Tallent, N. (1958). On individualizing the psychologist's clinical evaluation. *Journal of Clinical Psychology, 14,* 243–245.

Terner, J., & Pew, W. L. (1978). *The courage to be imperfect.* New York: Hawthorn Books.

Trachtenberg, J. (1961). *Jewish magic and superstition.* Cleveland & Philadelphia: Meridian Books and Jewish Publication Society.

Wachtel, P. L. (1977). *Psychoanalysis and behavior therapy.* New York: Basic Books.

Weeks, G. R., & L'Abate, L. (1982). *Paradoxical psychotherapy.* New York: Brunner/Mazel.

Weiss, L. (1986). *Dream analysis in psychotherapy.* New York: Pergamon Press.

Wexberg, E. (1970). *Individual Psychological treatment.* B. H. Shulman, Ed. Chicago: Alfred Adler Institute. (Original work published 1929.)

Wiesel, E. (1972). *Souls on fire: Portraits and legends of Hasidic masters.* New York: Random House.

Wolfe, W. B. (1932). *How to be happy though human.* London: Routledge & Kegan Paul.

Wolpe, J. (1958). *Psychotherapy by reciprocal inhibition.* Stanford, CA: Stanford University Press.

Wolpe, J. (1965). *The case of Mrs. Schmidt.* [Audiotape]. (Available from Counselor Recordings and Tests, Nashville, TN).

Index

TACTICS IN COUNSELING AND PSYCHOTHERAPY
Edited by John Beasley
Production supervision by Kim Vander Steen
Cover design by Lucy Lesiak Design, Park Ridge, Illinois
Composition by Point West, Inc., Carol Stream, Illinois
Paper, Finch Opaque
Printed and bound by McNaughton & Gunn, Saline, Michigan